Mental Toughness

*How You Can Develop Unstoppable
Self-Discipline, Willpower and
Success Habits By Adopting A
Champion's Mindset and the
Principles of Stoicism*

Contents

Part 1: Mental Toughness

Unlock the Spartan within You and Develop Relentless Self-Discipline, A Champion's Mindset, Unbeatable Willpower, and Powerful Success Habits

Introduction

We can define success as the accomplishment of a purpose or an aim. If we analyze our lives, we will quickly realize that each of us is trying to achieve success in one or more aspects of our lives and that those aspects - as well as our targets - keep changing with time.

For some of us, success may relate to losing weight while for others, it may be about getting a well-paying job, starting a business, etc. The crux of the matter is that we set different goals from time to time, and then strive towards fulfilling them. Several factors influence our ability to solve the success equation.

To succeed in whichever venture you undertake, you need positivity, creativity, perseverance, confidence, skills, potential, and a plethora of other ingredients necessary for the creation of success.

Among these factors, one stands apart from the rest, and many experts even acknowledge it as the number 1 key to being successful in any aspect of your life.

Do you know what I am referring to? Make a wild guess. A champion like you can easily figure that out. Yep, you got it right: I am talking about *mental toughness,* aka *"grit."*

If you are still wondering how grit relates to success or how it helps you become victorious in every journey you embark on, just ask yourself the following questions:

1. Are you sick and tired of working hard but not getting your desired results?

2. Have you endlessly tried other solutions, but nothing seems to work for more than a few weeks?

3. Do you finally want to say goodbye to making temporary sacrifices and discover something that works for you?

If so, then you have come to the right place.

The truth is that if you put your mind to it, you can achieve everything, even goals that may seem impossible to achieve right now. The goals you have set in life are not too big or impractical for you; neither is a lack of talent that has kept you from achieving the goals you have set but failed to achieve. A lack of mental toughness is the impediment on your pathway to success. The problem is not your goals or your lack of talent or passion. The problem is that you have thus far not realized that a lack of grit is the root cause of the issue.

If you struggle to accomplish a goal, it is because you do not realize the immense effort that goes into the process of accomplishing a goal, and because of this, you often give in to your temptations.

Accomplishing any target requires an incredible amount of self-discipline; when you become mentally tough, self-discipline is what you nurture. Studies prove that mental toughness directly relates to the success of a project.

To understand this better, think about how you treat a goal after setting it.

1. Do you feel highly enthusiastic about it at the start, but notice your motivation slowly diminishing with each passing day?

2. Do you set incredible goals for yourself, think and dream big, and think of making a difference in the world, but somehow fall short of doing that every time?

3. Do you often find yourself giving into temptations whenever it is time for you to work?

4. Do you doubt your confidence, abilities, and talent, and worry about whether you will make it to the finish line?

5. Do you find yourself making the same mistakes time and again, and have built a sort of a pattern?

6. Do you feel the universe is conspiring against you and keeping you from achieving your goals as fast as you would like to achieve them?

7. Do you lose your calm under pressure, find it difficult to compose yourself, and focus on the task?

If you answered two or more of these queries with a yes, it is likely you lack the mental toughness you need to be the boss of your life.

Even if you have answered yes to two or more of the above questions, there is nothing to worry about or fear. You are a champion in the making, and very soon, you will be exactly where you want to be in life after having achieved all your goals.

Do you know why and how I am sure of that?

For starters, you are here, reading this book. This alone is proof that shows your determination to prove yourself and your eagerness to learn about how you can fulfill all your dreams and goals.

The fact that you invested in this book shows you are ready to bring a remarkable change in your life and are just in search of the right tools and life strategies that will help you reclaim and transform your life!

Here is just a tiny fraction of what you will discover in this book:

• An understanding of what a strong mentality is as well as its comparison with weak mentality; you will learn about the crucial differences, pitfalls, mistakes, as well as how to spot and to avoid them

• How to perform under pressure and deal with setbacks: how the pros do it

• How to implement the 40% rule of mental toughness in your life

• How to cultivate emotional strength, a sense of purpose, and direction in life

• How to get over fear and anxiety

• Self-discipline: what it means, what it takes, how to get it

• A Champion's Mindset: how the world's winners think

• The comfort zone: find yours, then expand it

• Iron-tough Willpower: how to train your willpower

• Habits of Successful people

• How to handle failure: bounce back, forge through, embrace the failures;

...and much, much more!

Take a second to imagine your goal; it can be anything you are extremely ambitious about and cannot make do without in your life anymore. Perhaps envisage starting your own lifestyle business, taking theater classes, or starting your own fitness training classes.

Think of anything you wish to actualize and then imagine how you will feel if you eventually achieve it. For a few moments, picture yourself embracing your goal, standing at the finish line and having everyone applaud your efforts. That feeling is sure to be that of immense pleasure, contentment, gratitude, and pride.

The truth is that you have all the talent, ambition, and potential you need to accomplish that ambition you just envisioned and any others you may have. The only thing you are missing right now is the right mindset, a mindset characterized by mental toughness, discipline, and optimism.

You have the power to push against all limits and break all odds, be it in terms of fitness, finance, professional chores, relationships, business, or anything else. You can do it all because you are a natural winner.

You just need to build the winner's mindset, which is what this guide aims to help you do. If you trust yourself and the knowledge packed in this guide, you will be amazed at how far it takes you in life.

Do not just sit and read this; also get up at this instant, make a fist pump and say, *"I can achieve all my goals, and I will do it."* Say it a few times and see how it creates a surge of optimism bubbling inside you. Now say, *"I am working towards my goals and achieving them with each passing minute."* Say it aloud and with deep conviction. C'mon, say it FIVE more times!

Do you notice a smile spreading on your face? Have you instantly started believing that you can do it? Are you now thinking of ideas on how to follow through with your goal, or do you now think that nothing stands in the way of you and your goal, and you can achieve it no matter what may come?

This is the power of chanting positive affirmations and of believing in yourself. To create and grow the mental toughness that can take you wherever you want to go in life and help you achieve any goal you set your heart on, you need the same self-belief. It is as simple as that, and if you follow through with the actionable steps in this book, how quickly you start embracing and achieving all your goals will amaze you.

Let us begin this journey that helps you realize your genuine ambitions and then actualize them for good.

Section 1

The Modern Spartan

If you want to fly, give up everything that weighs you down.

To date, Spartan soldiers remain exemplary models of mental toughness. If you have read up on Greek mythology or watched Spartan-based movies, you are aware of the toughness of their training routine.

Boys supposed to become Spartan soldiers would be taken away from their mothers after turning seven years old. They would then be placed in schools called agōgē and taught how to read, write, sing, and dance, and they received education on their history.

The main discipline of training was their mental and physical strength and endurance. They were underfed and still trained on an empty stomach to build their stamina and inner resilience. This taught them how to fight and to persevere and keep going forward under extreme conditions. If they wanted more food, the boys had permission to steal but received severe punishment for being caught. This helped them develop stealth skills that would come in handy during times of war.

They had just one garment to cover themselves, moving around barefooted to toughen up the soles of their feet so they could move faster. They would normally complete their schooling when they turned 16, and their training would be complete when they reached age 20. At this point, they were considered completely ready to fight enemies.

I understand that the Spartan training seems extreme, and we would not want to consider the same for us, but we cannot deny that this training also helped them inculcate the necessary grit, resilience, and mental strength they needed to battle any enemy and obstacle.

If you look closely at the training that U.S. marines go through, you will realize that it too is not very different from that of the Spartans.

Mental toughness does not come without pushing your boundaries, exposing yourself to new challenges, and then compelling yourself to stay patient through these tests and to endure them with perseverance instead of surrendering to the pressure.

While you do not necessarily need to endure such extreme hardships as those experienced by Spartan Soldiers or US marines, you need to train yourself to understand the fact that *"there is no gain without pain."*

Arnold Schwarzenegger, the successful Austrian American bodybuilder, actor, filmmaker, politician, entrepreneur, and author, did not reach the stature of the Governor of California or enjoyed magnificent success just because he's Schwarzenegger. His interviews explicitly show that when he was training to become a bodybuilder, he would spend hours in the gym and would work out even harder when his muscles became sore.

This proves that there is no gain without putting in some pain first and that everything comes at a price. The cost of your success is your comfort right now, and if you wish to be the most successful version of yourself, you need to be ready to pay that price right now. This sounds harsh, but once you get the taste of success and overcome one obstacle, you will build the momentum for your success and will just keep going.

What exactly is mental toughness, and what does it encompass? Let us find out right here right now.

Understanding Mental Toughness

You must have heard this old age adage *"When the going gets tough, the tough get going,"* "right? As cliché as it sounds, it is at the very core of the field of sports psychology and psychology in general.

To achieve their set goals, Athletes must go through thousands of hours of tough and grueling mental and physical training. All of us need training of this sort, the kind that helps us unlock our true potential and overcome all our inner obstacles.

There is a champion locked within all of us. We are all warriors fighting the many impediments around us. We have that inner talent, that potential, that spark that is waiting for us to tap into it, and we can do that only if we work on becoming mentally tough.

Mental toughness *"is your capacity as an individual to deal well with the challenges, pressures, and stressors all around you that in one way or another debilitate your confidence and courage."* Once you can tackle and defeat all those obstacles, you perform at the very best of your ability, and regardless of any challenges, you are likely to emerge victorious in the end.

Experts also describe mental toughness as *"our ability to deal with all the problems that keep us from achieving a certain target."* Mental toughness is not the only factor that determines the chances of success.

While there are other elements at play, too, **studies have repeatedly proven that mental toughness alone accounts for around 25%** of your total variation in a certain performance. This shows why mental toughness so significantly influences your chances of success. Moreover, mental toughness improves your ability to perform well under pressure irrespective of the prevailing circumstances around you.

If you are mentally tough, you take full accountability of your performance. Instead of shrugging your shoulders and nodding your head in refusal every time you encounter a setback, you exhibit a true can-do attitude. Once you set your eyes on a goal, there is no looking back for you. Come what may, you choose to power through and do not blame your setbacks on circumstances. You know you are the real driver of your life's carriage, and you take full responsibility for that. You are aware of what challenges surround you, the journey you have committed yourself to, and the reward you will enjoy once you complete the journey to the end. This motivates you to look ahead and to keep moving forward.

Nobody has ever had it easy in life, even the ones you think came into this world with a silver spoon in their mouths. Everyone has his or her share of struggles to combat, and if someone makes it to the finish line, mental toughness is likely to be the element that determines this. Mental toughness instills in you the courage to handle your challenges instead of succumbing to the pressure.

Oftentimes, when we encounter a tensile situation, one that is not favorable towards our plans and end goals, our first reaction is to fret and panic. Sweat droplets appear on our foreheads, our eyebrows crunch, we bite our lips, and before we realize it, we are in a negative overthinking mindset that then triggers analysis paralysis. We become panic-stricken and strongly consider fleeing our goals. Many of us even quit our goals during such times only have regrets laden on our backs.

In all such instances, our ability to stay calm, think things through, aim to get a better perspective of things - and focus on the bigger picture - is the only thing that can help us respond better to the tricky situation so that we can make an informed decision. This ability is not automatic; it is a result of mental toughness.

Our level of mental toughness directly influences our ability to succumb to challenges or to take on them like a pro. Mental toughness serves more like a connecting link between stress management and peak performance because you can only function optimally when you learn how to deal effectively with your challenges, obstacles, and stressors.

Oftentimes, we use the term resilience interchangeably with mental toughness. While the two concepts are similar, they are not the same. Resilience, aka hardiness, is in terms of commitment, challenge, and control. Resilience is important because, to stay true to your commitment, you need to remain committed towards a cause so that you can control your nerves in case you are confronted by a challenge.

Mental toughness is almost the same with the slight difference of confidence in the equation. To get the perfect mental toughness recipe, you need to mix in self-confidence with the challenge, commitment, and control to tackle your challenges confidently and never lose faith in your abilities.

Research carried out by the Psychology Department at the University of Hull led by Dr. Peter Cough, (C Psych), shows that mental toughness comprises of four main ingredients also colloquially referred to as the "Four Cs," namely *confidence, control, challenge,* and *commitment.*

If you are confident of yourself and the cause you believe in, when avalanches of troubles befall you, you will keep your emotions and impulses in control, face challenges like a pro, and embrace your commitment for good, and you will become mentally tough.

When you are mentally tough, you are unstoppable because there is absolutely nothing that can keep you from being the winner you are. You are a beacon of hope, courage, and strength, one that should always shine bright. Since you believe in yourself, you only move forward with grace and prove your mettle to the world around you.

This is how Spartan soldiers functioned. While their stories may seem very inspirational to you, you may have an annoying voice inside you that keeps telling you how you cannot be mentally strong or confident like a Spartan. If that is the case, you are wrong. All of us can be the modern, more revolutionized and digitally equipped version of the Spartans.

How to Unleash the Modern Spartan within You

We all have dreams, ambitions, and desires, but not all of us dig deeper into them, explore them, or create goals centered on them.

With that noted, there is that one fine morning in our lives when we decide to do something purely for ourselves, something that adds meaning to our lives. We feel excited about finally pursuing what we want. We are brimming with energy and enthusiasm.

We plan the goal and the journey that takes us to it, and we even commit ourselves to writing down the goal. We embark on that journey with fervor and zest.

In the start, since we feel high-spirited, nothing seems impossible, and we feel capable of accomplishing a milestone or two. Soon enough, though, our wildest fears come true when we confront a gigantic obstacle.

We become panicky! Fear overcomes us, and we start considering the possibility of giving up on our goal. Before we realize it, we silently bid adieu to the goal and make the excuse of not feeling connected to the goal. While it is true that we can feel disconnected from our goals at times, our inability to battle our challenges is what keeps us from persevering. We give in to the pressure the minute the going gets tough. We then embark on another journey while deep inside, we still yearn for that goal we left and worry about the sentiments attached to it.

We worry about how we can never accomplish our deepest ambitions. We fret about how we give in to obstacles. Every time we think about how we never nail our goals even though we have the potential to do so, we feel pained from within.

While this scenario is common in relation to our genuine desires, ambitions, and goals, we behave in a similar manner when it comes to our routine tasks as well.

Every time we face a difficult task, we switch over to an easier option. Just because it is easier to work on a certain project, we do not try to take a more difficult one that can lead to greater rewards and returns. Just because we are used to living a certain lifestyle, we do not experiment with new approaches to see what suits us better. Just because working out for 45 minutes seems difficult, we continue with our 20-minute workout routine and become comfortable with our current weight even though it is not our target weight. This is how many of us function, and therefore, many of us feel unfulfilled with our lives.

1. Have you ever thought about why your life lacks structure and meaning?

2. Do you ever worry about how people around you describe you?

3. Have you ever thought about what your goals mean to you?

4. Do you fret about why you never accomplish anything, but only plan things?

5. Do you think about how others around you reach the peak of the mountain while you struggle with hiking even midway?

Well, the answer to these questions boils down to a lack of mental toughness. If you worry more about nurturing that virtue and less about giving in to the pressures around you, you too will unleash your true potential. Becoming a modern version of a Spartan is not difficult at all; it just requires a tad bit of extra effort, and if you do just that, you will have the power to actualize every goal.

When you decide to put in the effort, you shall stop worrying about quitting your goal. You will stop questioning your worth and capabilities. You will stop doubting your potential and power. You will stop giving in to your fears. You will stop allowing your struggles and obstacles to get the better of you. You will stop empowering your fears and problems. You will stop letting your pressures define you. You will overcome your lack of confidence, strength, control, commitment, and perseverance, and you will learn how to power through challenges.

Now that you have heard about the story of Spartan warriors, have you wondered about how difficult it must have been for a Spartan soldier to walk barefooted for miles? We cannot even walk for a few steps like that; our feet would ache too much soon after. Just imagine how Spartan warriors would have gone barefooted on pathways strewn with rocks.

Have you also wondered about how tough it must have been to fight on an empty stomach, and yet, when we do not eat for a few hours, we feel incapacitated, incapable of doing anything at all?

Have you pondered upon how Spartans kept going despite all the hardships they encountered and the fierce training they had to endure to bear the honor of becoming Spartan warriors? They could have complained too, but they chose not to because their goal was clear. Unlike Spartan warriors, when many of us encounter even tiny troubles, we decide to sleep on our ambitions for good.

Yes, times have changed, and we do not have to comply with certain rules or a grueling training schedule, because unlike Spartans, we have at our disposal many tools, approaches, methodologies, and technologies we can use to make things easier for us.

In the technology-driven, fast-paced world we live in, achieving our goals is not too difficult. We have the digital tools - along with lots of training - to inculcate the soft skills we require to actualize any dream into reality. All we need to get started and be well on our way to achieving one milestone after another is mental toughness.

The Spartans did not have things the easy way; we do. Yes, we have struggles of our own, and our challenges are completely different, but we also have many ways and approaches we can use to ease that pain. If we stop empowering our fears and allow our courage to grow bigger, we can be the finest version of ourselves. Yes, you can do it, and this book tells you exactly how to do it.

How this Handy Guide Helps You

If you are expecting a fairy godmother to appear out of thin air and with the flick of her magic wand around your head, turn you into the most successful version of yourself, you are living in your fantasies because inasmuch as many of us may want that to happen, it only happens in Hollywood films.

However, and this is very important, do you know that you have a magic wand that you can use to turn yourself into any version you want? Each of us has a magical power that we can tap into and use to transform ourselves into whomever we want to be.

Sadly, not many of us realize that we possess this power, which is why we never use it. There is a trick factor attached to finding our power. You need to build it yourself, but once you do that, there will be no going back for you. The magical power is mental toughness. This book teaches you how to design that wand from scratch.

Here is an overview of how this book will help you in that regard.

What This Book Teaches You

Here is a small sampling of the many invaluable lessons you will learn from this handy guide.

1. **The Strong Mentality versus Weak Mentality:** the crucial differences between the two, the pitfalls, as well as how to identify and avoid some common mistakes. In this section, you will learn about the differences between a weak and strong mindset/mentality. After reading this section, you will have a clear idea of what distinguishes a weak mindset from a strong, powerful one, and exactly what you need to do to nurture the latter.

• **Performing Well under Pressure and Dealing with Setbacks:** how the pros do it. This part of the book talks about how the mind can falter under pressure and cause you to fail, flounder, or make bad decisions such as abdicating the pursuit of your goals. You will also learn about how to stay composed during high-pressure situations and how not to give the undesirable circumstances the ability to sway you away from your mission. Using real-life examples of accomplished people, you will learn the importance of keeping calm when in tricky situations, and the right way to take on your challenges.

• **The 40% rule of mental toughness:** This section discusses the 40% rule of mental toughness, a rule that means there is a lot more left "in the tank," and that even when your body/mind is telling you that you are at your limit, you are actually only at 40% so keep going! People who push past that 40% are the ones who succeed.

• **Emotional strength, sense of purpose, and direction:** In this part, you will learn about the importance of emotional strength and intelligence in your life, as well as how emotional strength shapes your mental toughness. You will learn about why you must have a clear purpose and reason for doing something so that your mental toughness and willpower has an anchor and direction. You will also learn about the importance of emotional strength in your life and the different forms it takes. This section also discusses how emotions influence and shape your success and failure, and how emotions associate with your willpower, which is an important ingredient of mental toughness.

• **Getting over fear and anxiety:** This section covers fear and the part it plays as an obstacle to mental toughness and success. You will learn about fear and its various types, including the one that keeps you safe from life-threatening situations and the one that keeps you from achieving success. You will also learn about how to discern between the two so that you can pay heed to the former but keep your distance from the latter. You will also learn about how anxieties and unnecessary fears give rise to self-doubt and how that keeps you from unleashing your true potential. Once you understand that, you will have the power, knowledge, and strategies you need to squash any fear.

• **Self-discipline: what it means, what it takes, and how to get it:** This section of the book shall illuminate the lives of the many successful people across the globe whom we admire, look up to, and seek inspiration and guidance from. When you read about how real-life people began from scratch, faced countless hurdles, and kept going, you will feel inspired to do the same for yourself. Moreover, their life, routines, and journeys shall help you comprehend the amount of effort that goes into shaping our success; this will help you understand that success never comes easy, which will help you stop looking for shortcuts to accomplish our objectives.

• **A Champion's Mindset: how do the world's winners think?** This section is all about real-life examples of successful men and women who have an iron-tough mentality and who practice excellent self-discipline. You will learn how warriors, survivors, and champions think, the kind of attitude they have, and how they go about their goals. Hearing about these will help you quit the whining attitude so that you can get started on doing.

• **The comfort zone: find yours, then expand it:** This section is all about how the comfort zone can restrict you and keep you from achieving your chief aims in life. There is no point in being mentally tough if you will keep staying within your comfort zone anyway. Mental toughness can help you bust the walls of the comfort zone. All of us have that zone where we feel at rest, and we do not like getting out of it. It is likely you have a comfort zone too that you feel extremely attached to. You do not wish to move past it because you feel nice and cozy. Well, just ask yourself this:

Has anyone ever accomplished something worthwhile by doing nothing? Can you ever move past the blizzard and embrace the sunshine at the end of the road if you keep snuggling in your blanket? The answer is no! This has never happened and will never happen. If you are serious about changing the course of your life for the better, you need to know exactly what is holding you back from bursting the walls. You need to acknowledge the setbacks and fears, and to face them courageously using actionable and practical steps that help you slowly expand your comfort zone and constantly prove to yourself that you can act despite fear or discomfort.

• **Iron-tough Willpower: how to train your willpower:** In this part of the book, you will learn about the connection between willpower, mental toughness, and the fulfillment of your goals. You will learn about how your willpower can be your tool against the part of your mind that fosters fear and self-doubt. In addition, you will learn about how to build, sustain, and improve your willpower so that you always have a good supply of it whenever you need it and especially during challenging moments of life.

• **Habits of Successful People:** Here, you will learn about the amazing habits of successful people as well as how adopting similar habits can contribute to your success and the accomplishment of your goals.

• **How to handle failure: bounce back, forge through, embrace the failures:** This section is all how to deal with setbacks and failure. Here, we shall talk about how failure is an inevitable part of all challenging journeys, and how experiencing failure is not a bad thing. Contrary to popular belief, failure does not mean you cannot achieve something; neither is it a testament of your incompetence. Failure is simply a glitch you need to embrace, understand,

and learn from as you move towards achieving your goals. This section also talks about actionable techniques you can use to overcome failures without letting them lower your morale so that you constantly build the willpower to take on challenges and soar high.

After reading this guide, you will know the A to Z of mental toughness and will feel strongly motivated, enthusiastic, and all charged for making a difference in your life. You will also know how to create a mental toughness plan that helps you become invincibly strong and mentally resilient.

Let us begin with an analysis and comparison of the strong mentality versus the weak mentality.

Section 2

Strong Mentality versus Weak Mentality

The Crucial Differences, Pitfalls, Mistakes, and How to Spot Them

> Never throughout history has a (wo)man who lived a life of ease left a name worth *remembering.*
>
> Theodore Roosevelt

Whether you are an athlete, a marketer, an educationist, an industrialist, an analyst, a writer, a designer, or are in any other profession, you have perhaps heard your mentors and industry experts advise that you nurture a strong mindset and forego a weak mentality. This is for a good reason.

A strong mindset is crucial to paving the way for your success and is exactly what helps you become mentally tough. You may be wondering, what is a strong mentality? What is the difference between a strong and a weak mentality? What perpetuates a weak mindset, and more importantly, how can I recognize and overcome the habits that lead to it?"

This section of the book will give you answers to these and other important questions you may have about a strong mindset.

Understanding the Strong and Weak Mentalities

If you like Star Wars, you are probably familiar with Anakin and his character traits. He strongly believes he can achieve anything. If you look at him that way, he nurtures a strong mentality because he has faith in his abilities.

However, he also lacks consistency, flexibility, and patience, which means he is likely to give up the minute kicking the ball becomes harder, and obstacles pour in. He does not endure hardships until he makes it to the finish line, which is why he never accomplishes anything. When you analyze his personality and mindset from this angle, it looks like he has a weak mentality. This shows that a strong mindset and mentality consists of several elements.

1. First, you need to have complete faith in your capabilities. You must realize and acknowledge that you are powerful, talented, and worthy of success and that if you keep investing effort in your cause, you will achieve it in the end.

2. Second, you need to be consistent in your efforts. Working 12 hours one day and not working at all for the next five days in a row will not get you anywhere. The output you achieve in one day will become neutral when you factor in the aspect of no yield at all over the next five days. Only by consistently putting in the effort do you yield a compound effect. This should tell you that constructive and desired results come from regular activity and meaningful action taken daily. This is part of what it means to be mentally tough.

Think of a time when you worked out in the gym daily for 30-60 minutes and made sure you ate a healthy diet. You lost four pounds in two weeks and felt elated at your performance. Think about how the minute you started eating cheeseburgers daily with no physical activity; you quickly gained back those four pounds. Had you consistently worked out for that week too and followed a healthy diet, it is likely you would have lost even more weight.

3. Third, you need to be flexible in how you approach and handle obstacles and goals. You must plan for your goals; you must have an action plan that complements your goals so that you know where you are heading, why you need to take a certain route, and what steps you need to take at what time. That notwithstanding, you do not

need to approach the plan with rigidity. You must factor in room for flexibility and changes.

Remember that the only thing constant in life is change; no matter what, change happens in one way or another. You may think sticking to your grueling training schedule will help you bag gold at the Olympics in the 100-meter dash category, but just when you seem about ready to achieve your aim, you slip while going down a flight of stairs and fracture your ankle. You may think you have the perfect marketing plan that will help your client and amount to a good profit for you but the next day, you find out about a new economic reform that is likely to minimize your profit margins significantly.

This is how life is: *unpredictable*, *risky*, and *tough*.

Problems come out of nowhere, take weird, frightening shapes, and try their best to knock you off the path to your goals. If you let them knock you down permanently, you are not mentally strong, are you? You need to challenge them back, and sometimes, the best way to do this is by adopting a flexible attitude towards your problem and the end goal.

It is okay to not know everything and to not have everything figured out beforehand. Sometimes, uncertainty is your biggest asset because it helps you mold yourself according to the situation. Every time you encounter a challenge, be ready to embrace it, and to change course according to it.

For instance, if you are unable to compete in the Olympics this year, perhaps it is because you would not have won this year. If you find out you need to have an additional degree to qualify for a scholarship grant, maybe it is an opportunity in disguise. When you become flexible, you stop fueling the problems and instead empower yourself.

4. Fourth, you need to be extremely patient when you begin the voyage towards your goals and success. Patience is a virtue not many have, which is why only those who truly possess it are able to move past the tunnel of darkness and step on the road of light. During your journey, you will encounter countless obstacles. Some of them will be small and manageable, but others shall be gigantic and intense. Some may even knock you down to the extent that you feel you may never get back up again; in such times, you need to power through.

Remember how Thomas Edison failed 9999 times at creating a successful invention; even after so many failures, he did not give up. Unfortunately, that is not the case with most of us; in fact, when many of us fail twice, we often surmise that the goal is not for us.

Even after failing 9999 times, Edison still yearned to create something meaningful, which is why he finally created the light bulb on his 10,000th try. That is what mental toughness and a strong mentality look like. He was patient; he persevered and proved his mettle. Later, he went on to patent all his other failed inventions and to turn them into successful products too.

The fact of the matter is that you need to be persistent when you approach a certain goal, and that to embrace your goal, you need to be able to persevere through the long-suffering that leads to the goal. This is not easy, but do not forget, *success is never easy.*

If you are impatient, if you often choose to give in to your hardships instead of persevering through them, if you act rigidly towards your goals and plans, and if you often take the easy road when the going gets tough, you are mentally weak.

If you do not put in the daily effort to achieve your goal, and most importantly, if you do not believe you are capable of achieving anything you put your mind to, and that your potential can always grow, you nurture a weak mentality. This kind of mentality will never help you accomplish anything in life.

Think of every time you chose to succumb to an obstacle and analyze the reason behind it. If you quit your goal of writing a book because you felt the time was not right, maybe you gave up on it because you lacked the consistency to write and research for it daily. If you decided to give up on an opportunity to work with a certain client, maybe it is because you were not flexible enough to embrace that slight change in your plans. If you decided to quit your MBA because you could not simultaneously handle the academic and professional workload, maybe you were not patient enough to wait for the fruitful outcome in the end. If you declined a potential client's project because you felt that the website development project was beyond your scope of work, maybe you did so because you did not have faith in your capabilities.

A lack of self-confidence, patience, flexibility, and consistency is usually what causes you to quit your goals; this also explains why you lack mental toughness. Let me clarify the distinction between a weak and strong mentality better with a detailed comparison of the two.

Strong Mentality versus Weak Mentality

The table below shows a detailed analysis and comparison of the two types of mentalities we have persistently talked about in this section. This comparison will help you get a better understanding of the two, which will help you comprehend the category you fall in.

Strong Mentality	Weak Mentality
You work hard to achieve what you set your eyes on and take full accountability of your commitments. In case you encounter setbacks, you do not play the blame game; you focus on what you want.	You have a bad habit of blaming others for your defeats and troubles. If you fall in this category, you are likely to believe that the entire world owes you happiness and success and that if you cannot achieve something, it is because the universe is out to get you; nothing is ever your fault.
You are courteous to people, but do not focus on pleasing others. You spend your time, energy, and effort working on your goals so that you can accomplish them as soon as possible. If you have a strong mentality, you worry less about what others think of you and pay more attention to improving your personality.	If you have a weak mentality, you seek attention and validation from others. In case you have a weak mentality, you are likely to go to great lengths to please others just so they like you because you find it difficult to accept rejection.

You are aware of your value and capabilities and have full faith in your potential, talents, and skills. If you have a strong mindset, you know your worth and care less about whether people value you because you value your own self, and you use that confidence to fuel your motivation to actualize your goals.	Since you are a people pleaser, you are desperate for approval and recognition. In case someone does not treat you as desired, you feel heart-broken and are unable to perform optimally.
Your self-belief empowers you, and while you know you are extraordinary, you are nonetheless aware that you need to focus on your self-improvement to become better. You adopt a self-reflective attitude and carry out regular introspection sessions that help you become more aware of your weaknesses so that you can overcome them and become a polished version of yourself. This is how you become mentally stronger and with time, move closer towards your goals.	While you yearn for validation from others, you are also self-indulged. It is difficult for you to accept your faults and weaknesses, and therefore you feel hurt when someone points them out. Your mindset is rich in negative and limiting beliefs that keep you from believing that growth comes with self-reflection and personal improvement.

You nurture a strong, optimistic, and growth-oriented mindset that helps you believe that talent and potential are improvable and that you can nurture any skill and belief you need to attract success into your life. You know you are worthy of achievement, and so you work harder to polish yourself so that you can enjoy great opportunities for growth.	You nurture a weak, fixed mindset that makes you believe you have an innate amount of talent that you cannot improve upon no matter what you do.
You are patient and are willing to stick to a commitment for the long haul. You enjoy the process that takes you towards all your goals and believe in being both goal-oriented and process-oriented. You focus on every step of the process and cherish it because that is what takes you to your destination.	Since you lack self-confidence, you do not believe you have in it you to achieve something. This makes you lose your focus on your goals, and you are likely to quit them even after setting them for the hundredth time.
Your mentally strong mindset encourages you to pursue delayed gratification instead of instant gratification. Since you always keep the bigger picture in mind, a setback or even a series of them does not upset you for very long. Every time you have the option of going	Since you do not have the patience and resilience to face and battle obstacles, you surrender to challenges quickly. Whenever you have the option of going for instant gratification, you grab it and bid adieu to your end goal. You demand immediate results, which is

for the easier option, you remind yourself of what you genuinely want and strive to achieve it.	why you never reach what you desperately want.
Since you are aware of the importance of your goals and you cherish and enjoy every step of the process, you focus on living in the present moment and embrace every minute of it. You dwell in the present and worry less about the future or past; this attitude helps you make efficient use of every moment. When you encounter a challenge, you worry less about the trouble the challenge is causing and focus more on how to resolve it so that you can achieve your goal.	Your lack of self-confidence and inability to concentrate on the end goal keeps you from living in the moment. You constantly rehash your past mistakes and failures, which keeps you from making good use of the present moment. Similarly, you also worry more about how things will pan out in the future, which keeps you from taking meaningful action in the present.
While you are dedicated to your growth and strongly believe in your capabilities, this does not keep you from celebrating other people's success and appreciating their strengths. You feel happy for others, and this positivity helps you draw others towards you.	Because you are a people pleaser, your self-indulgent nature and inability to achieve something keeps you from wishing other people well. Every time you see someone progressing in life, you secretly hope for that person to falter and fail.

Since you have many goals and commitments to fulfill, you enjoy being alone so that you can assess and examine your improvement and work towards actualizing your goals.	You fear being alone because that makes you recall your struggles and failures; therefore, you always want to around others.
Like everybody else, you enjoy achieving your goals, but that does not keep you from nurturing an optimistic attitude towards risks and challenges in life. Struggles and challenges upset you, yes, but you do not allow them to worry you for long. Instead of losing hope, you embrace change and focus on turning challenges into opportunities.	Your lack of faith in yourself makes you fearful of change. Since you are sure you can never achieve anything on your own, you become reluctant about risks and changes, which is why you panic every time a struggle comes your way.
In addition to being optimistic, you are also aware of your own emotions. You understand your emotions and use them to manage the situations around you effectively. Instead of reacting to your intense, volatile emotions, you sit with them until you understand them, a factor that helps you respond to the situation better. If encountering a failure makes you feel angry, you do not let anger cause you to make a	You never focus on understanding your emotions or seeking self-awareness. You react to your emotions, jump to conclusions, and even allow other people to influence your emotions, decisions, and life. If someone says you should opt for a career in marketing because it pays well, you ignore the fact that you want to pursue your passion for arts.

hasty decision. Instead, you allow yourself to calm down and later think things through. This ability also helps you understand the emotions of others and easily manage people around you. You are often the one pacifying intense arguments between others.	
While you strive for excellence and your goals, it does not keep you from acknowledging and enjoying what you have. You feel grateful for your blessings and live a content life.	You do not work towards accomplishing your aims, nor do you feel thankful for what you have. Even if you have every luxury around you, you yearn for something more because you are dissatisfied with your own self.
You know you can only control your thoughts, attitude, and actions; everything else is beyond your control. This helps you focus on what you can manage and to let go of everything you cannot control or improve. If people do not treat you well, instead of crying over how they do not love you, you distance yourself from them. If new competitors rise in the	You expect everything to be within your control, which is why you lose your calm when things fail to pan out as planned or as intended. Since you expect the world to owe you, you wish for everyone to obey your commands, but since this is not how the world functions, you feel frustrated. In addition, you pay less attention to how you can control your own

marketplace, giving you a hard time to grab a higher market share, you do not wish for them to vanish into thin air. Instead, you focus on how to improve your product to regain your lost market share.	thoughts and worry more about others.

Now that you know what separates a strong mindset from a weak one, you can check your behavior and personality for these character traits and use this analysis to understand the type of mentality you possess at this moment.

How to Know If You Have a Weak Mindset

If you have long struggled with achieving your targets, if you often set goals one day and forget all about them a week later, if you surrender to instant gratification in whatever form it comes to you in, are impatient to stick to a goal for the long haul, you have a weak mindset.

If you give in to your struggles every time they come your way, have zero faith in your capabilities, focus more on managing others and less on controlling your thoughts positively, if you worry about what others think of you and not about how you can improve, and if you blame others for your failures, you have a weak mindset.

This weak mindset keeps you from doing everything you have ever wanted. It could be keeping you from self-publishing a book and effectively marketing it to turn it into a huge success. It could be keeping you from creating your own ad agency to pursue your passion for advertising. It could be keeping you from working on a cause for the transgender community.

This weak mindset could be keeping you from building a healthy and active lifestyle, so you stay fit and avoid health issues. It could be keeping you from planting organic vegetables in your kitchen garden and slowly growing your own produce.

This weak mindset could be keeping you from expanding your legal firm from a small setup to a huge firm that can help more people. It could be keeping you from creating and selling your own fitness programs to build a career out of your skillset and ambition. A weak mindset is the one keeping you from achieving these goals and several other similar goals that you consistently give up on because you lack the mental strength and stamina to stick to your goals until the very end.

While you may again blame the universe for meddling in your fate and not letting you become successful, the truth is that you are to blame for this. Fortunately, you can do something about the situation.

You can start by acknowledging that you have a weak mentality; you can then admit how that mentality negatively influences your life.

Next, you need to identify the weak and unconstructive habits you have that, in one way or another, strengthen your weak mindset. You need to break those habits so that you can then slowly replace your weak mindset with a strong one that helps you achieve your goals.

How to Recognize and Break Habits that Contribute to a Weak Mindset

Dedicate 30-60 minutes of your day to self-observation. Look at how you behave with others, how you tackle and treat your obstacles and goals, and how you perceive the challenges that make up your life.

If you have any of the following habits, it is time to break them for good and replace them with positive ones.

#1: You feel sorry for yourself

It is okay to feel bummed out occasionally. It is even okay to feel angry, lonely, and sad.

However, if you feel sorry for yourself and if you repeatedly engage in self-pity or in thinking of why you are doomed for life, you have a habit of feeling sorry for yourself. This habit contributes to your negative and weak mindset and keeps you from becoming mentally tough.

How to Overcome this Habit:

To break this unhealthy habit, first, become more conscious of it. Be specifically aware of the usage of phrases and terms such as "I am always alone," "I feel miserable," "Nobody is there to help me," "Nobody cares about me," and similar words in your internal and external language.

If you consistently use such words and phrases, and if you often feel bad for not being able to do things instead of focusing on how to achieve your targets, you have this bad habit.

Next, you need to work on your self-talk to make it more positive so that you can stop pitying yourself. Every time you find yourself engaging in self-pity, acknowledge that you feel sorry for yourself and then write down the statements you used. Go over these statements and analyze them in the light of the realistic and fast-paced world we live in today. We achieve our goals when we work hard for them. If you, too, want the best, you need to put in your best effort too.

With this realization, replace your pitiful suggestion with something more positive and uplifting. Say things such as "My goal may be difficult, but I can and will achieve it," "I love myself, and when I am happy with myself, I draw positivity towards myself," and "I care for my needs and work to fulfill them."

After creating it, loudly repeat a positive suggestion several times aloud and then after every few hours. Work on all the negative statements in your self-talk and turn them into positive ones. If you do this consistently, you will always build the habit of positively talking to yourself and will break the self-pitying habit.

#2: You give away your power

We often forget that we have control over our lives and that we possess the power to shape things the way we want. In addition to forgetting this, we also end up giving away our power to others by letting them make decisions for us and by getting angry with them for not doing things our way.

First, you need to make your own decisions and then take full accountability for them. It is your life; you need to be in charge of it! With that said, if you do not take a stand for yourself, and if you always nod in agreement with what others direct you to do, you will never feel empowered.

Secondly, understand that nobody owes you anything. If you decide to make a certain move, take full accountability for it because that move was and will remain your decision; you need to own up to that.

If you stop taking responsibility for your life and decisions, you will expect people to do things for you, and you will become a pushover. You will hand over your power to them and later cry over spilled milk.

How to Overcome this Habit:

If you keep expecting things to become better for you automatically, for people to oblige to your commands, and for your life to improve on its own, it is because you give your power to others and do not take accountability for your life and decisions. To overcome this habit, do the following:

1. Analyze your life in detail and pick out all the decisions you have made recently because someone asked you to do so.

2. Assess the implications of those decisions as well as how things panned out for you.

3. If you were not too pleased with the decision, but obliged to the command and accepted the result because you do not have the power to decide things for yourself, wrap your head around the fact that things will never be great for you because you will always fail to own up to your life.

4. If you want your life to be meaningful and valuable, take accountability of your life now.

5. Create a powerful, positive suggestion centered on that aspect, such as "This is my life. I take full responsibility for it and will work hard to make it as pleasant and meaningful as I want." Chant this 10 times with confidence and conviction and make sure to practice

it twice daily. This rewires your brain to think optimistically and to become responsible for your life.

6. Just go through the current state of your life and pick out any top three areas you would like to structure and improve on first. For instance, you can pick health, wealth, and spirituality.

7. Now analyze those areas and figure out the issues in each aspect.

8. List down all the changes you want to make in those areas and pick any one that you would like to work on immediately. For instance, if you are not happy with your financial situation and your need of the hour is to find a job that pays at least twice as much as you are earning now, put that as your topmost goal.

9. You now need to work towards that target, and with each passing day, remind yourself to work harder until you fulfill it.

Together, these nine action steps shall help you focus more on a clearer goal and nurture the mental toughness you need to become the true, powerful boss of your life.

#3: You fail to focus on the moment

Mentally weak people are in the bad habit of dwelling in the past or in the future. If you wish to become a champion in your life, but you also think this wish is far from actualization, it is likely that you never embrace the moment. This means you always complain about what you do not have, rehash the past and imagine the worst-case scenarios long before you achieve an outcome.

You do nothing to improve the situation in the present moment or to live a better life today. This is why you never take any meaningful action in the moment, and why you only whine about how you never have enough time to do things.

How to Break this Habit:

If you are tired of complaining, and if you want to get things done, become more mindful and appreciative of the present moment.

Different challenges that come from time to time are only a test of your willingness to change, to adjust to those struggles, and to stretch your limits. If you ignore them or procrastinate and fail to develop effective solutions to tackle them, you will only increase your misery.

You need to focus your efforts on improving the present moment so that you do not lose things you can attain and sustain. Focusing on the here and now (the present) helps you realize the power you have over things.

Here is how you cultivate a deeper awareness of the present moment.

1. Take a goal you have decided to work on and break it into smaller milestones. If you feel that the goal shall take around two months to accomplish, break the goal into milestones of two weeks each so that every two weeks you have certain targets to fulfill.

2. Take every milestone and list down the activities you need to do to achieve it. If your 2-week milestone is to start a blog and to create content for it, your activities would include choosing the topic and blog name. These activities should also include deciding whether to create a WordPress blog yourself or to hire someone to do it for you, selecting the medium on which to build the blog, creating a list of blog-post ideas for it, getting a domain name and so on.

3. For every activity, list down sub-activities you must carry out to complete that activity. Write down what you need to do at what time and how you should execute it.

4. Make sure to peg every task to a time and date so that you know by when you need to have completed it. Write down how much time every task should take so that you do not spend hours and days doing something menial.

5. Once the list is ready, review it a couple of times and then pick anything you can work on right away.

6. Start that task without any delay and pay attention to every tiny step of the process. For instance, if your first task is to research for blog ideas and you think it should only take two hours daily to you decide on the right topic, get started with it now. Pay attention to how you research online, the ideas that run in your head, and the excitement you feel. This engages you in the task and helps you focus better in the moment instead of thinking of the past or future.

7. Once you complete the task, take a break if you have one scheduled. If you feel you can work on another task, or if it is time to work on one, do it.

8. Similarly, work on your To-do list in this manner so that you engage in productive work for six to ten hours daily.

9. Moreover, try to focus better on everything you do in the moment, even if it is something as simple as resting. We often wander off in negative thoughts when our minds do not have any mental preoccupations. This causes us to dwell in the past or future and keeps us from enjoying the present moment and utilizing it effectively. If you are cooking a meal, enjoy its aroma, focus on how you stir the ladle in the pot and pay attention to how you prepare the

ingredients. If you are dusting the table, pay attention to how the duster moves smoothly on the table, and wipes off dust. This helps you engage better in a task, which helps you enjoy it more so that you make every moment count and worry less about what happened or what may happen.

#4: You fail to embrace adversity

A lack of mental strength keeps you from perceiving your obstacles positively. Every time a struggle comes your way, you do your best to flee it to escape the misery.

The reason why you do not have any accolades or accomplishments to your credit is not that you are incapable. It is because you lack the right attitude to work towards it, an attitude that includes not seeing your obstacles as the stepping-stones to success.

How to Improve this Habit:

To move from being the HR Manager to the HR Executive, to get web designing clients so that you can go from $50 per project to $300 per project, to go from selling ten eBooks per month to selling a 3000 monthly, and to go from having 28% body fat to only 10%, you need to embrace adversity. To achieve every goal, you have ever set in your life, you need to embrace adversity.

Here is what you should do to embrace adversity and keep moving forward:

1. Every time you encounter an obstacle or challenge, try to keep your calm and wits about you. When adversity strikes and you realize that things are not going to pan out as planned, take deep breaths. Inhale through your nose to a count of five, exhale to a count of seven, and repeat this ten times. When you exhale for longer than you inhale,

you flush out your stress and feel calmer within a couple of minutes.

2. In a few minutes, you will feel calmer than before.

3. When you feel more relaxed, go through your obstacle again. You will now think clearly and will understand the obstacle better. The situation that earlier seemed like a huge monster will appear less damaging to you now. That is because you have changed your emotional state from one of frenzy, panic, and negativity to one of calmness and positivity.

4. Analyze the situation and identify the threats attached to it. If you have lost a client, what are the negatives associated with it? Next, think of what you can do to improve the situation. In case you have lost a client due to poor service, acknowledge your weakness and think of ways to get that client back or maybe pacify the situation by apologizing.

5. Think of any positives associated with the apparent setback. Even if it is something potentially harmful, you are likely to find something good associated with it too. For instance, if you have lost a client, maybe that instance helped you understand your brand's weaknesses better so that you can improve. If you have an urgent order to fulfill, perhaps that is your chance to prove your worth. Once you change your perspective towards it, the adversity seems more like an opportunity.

Work on these steps gradually and consistently, and you will develop the strength to perceive adversities positively. If a problem is too fierce in nature, you can take a few hours or even a day off from thinking about it. Do something enjoyable for some time, and when you feel better, resume your work.

#5: You fail to challenge yourself

The great Albert Einstein once said, *"One should not pursue goals that are easily achieved. One must develop an instinct for what one can just barely achieve through one's greatest efforts."*

This golden rule is one followed by all the mentally tough and accomplished people in the world, and if you are to become mentally strong, too, you need to embrace and follow Einstein's wise words.

Since you lack the mental toughness you need to achieve your goals, you need to build an instinct for what you can barely accomplish through your greatest efforts.

If you lack mental toughness, it is because you have a bad habit of underestimating yourself simply because you lack self-belief. If you now feel determined to actualize your goals irrespective of whether that goal is to start your own Etsy store selling paper crafts and turn it into a thriving business, or it is to complete your law degree and work as an associate in the top law firm in the city, you need to start challenging yourself.

How to Overcome the Habit:

To start challenging yourself so that you can better uncover and explore your capabilities as well as polish them, here is what you should do:

1. Make sure you push yourself to accomplish your set goal in the designated time. If you have decided to achieve a goal in two months, make sure you work on the plan of action consistently so that you actualize your goals within the set time.

2. As you progress towards your goal or smaller milestone, try to challenge yourself by achieving the target

in less time. If you have a deliverable due in two days, try to achieve it in one day. If you must write a report in five hours, try to do it in three hours. When you do this, you constantly challenge yourself to become more productive and achieve more in less time.

3. Once you achieve a target, set another goal related to it, and try to ensure that the new target is more complex than the previous one. For instance, if your previous goal increased your e-store sales by 10%, try to challenge yourself to increase it by 30% the next month. When you do this, you will consistently challenge yourself to move a step further every time.

4. Have something to look forward to every day, and consistently push yourself to achieve it every day. Once you do this, set a goal to do even better or work on a tougher target the next time.

If you work using this approach, you will soon break free from your cocoon of negativity and emerge as a confident, happier, and mentally tougher version of yourself.

#6: You do not think, act, and respond positively to struggles

Sadly, we cannot control everything in our lives. Unfortunately, only a select few of us realize and accept this truth, especially in times when things take an unexpected twist, and everything goes berserk.

Try to retrace the first thoughts that pop into your mind every time you face a struggle such as trying to set up your own WordPress website and failing every time, failing to get freelancing gigs, hearing from an expert musician that you are a terrible singer, or losing a job you loved.

The thoughts and the behavior you show at such instances are likely to be negative, especially if you have not made it too far in life in terms of growth. If you do not want your struggles to get the better of you, you need to stop acting that way.

How to Overcome this Habit:

Whatever you wish to accomplish, be it starting your own drop-shipping business or organizing a fantastic art exhibition where you sell all the art you have created over the past few months, you need to inculcate the habit of thinking and acting positively. You are the boss of your mind; the sooner you accept this, the better you will start acting.

Nobody but you can fix your problems. Each person has his or her mess to take care of and struggles to battle. You are your only savior, and only you have the ability and potential to escape your troubles if you approach them positively. Here is how you can do that.

1. Be conscious of your thoughts and quickly swap a negative thought with a positive one; we looked at how to do this earlier.

2. Stop attaching labels such as "bad," "troubles," "difficulties," "terrible," and the likes to undesirable situations. If you feel stuck in a rut, describe the situation for what it is. If you have an urgent, bulk order to fulfill and suddenly, you are under-staffed, do not describe it as *trouble*. Instead, describe it as a case where you need to fulfill an order that is difficult to do because you have less staff to manage it. When you stop describing a difficult situation as a "bad" or "problematic" situation and instead start describing it in detail for what it really is, you eliminate the undue negativity and fear attached to the

problem, which helps you adopt a more realistic attitude towards it.

3. Next, analyze the situation and enlist its pros or cons, good or bad points. Be as unbiased as possible. Treat the learning outcomes as good points and the tricky parts as the bad points. Continuing with the earlier example, the bad point can be that you are understaffed, but the good point can be to find out whether you can manage the problem singlehandedly and prove your mettle.

4. Take a time-out from all the excessive worrying by doing something calming and fun. For instance, if you find out that the weather forecast has shifted from sunny to rainy on the day of your outdoor event, take a few deep breaths, and watch something funny. Focus on that throughout the 10 minutes and constantly bring your attention back to the funny clip instead of worrying about the problematic situation at hand. If you do this a few times, you will learn to focus better on one task at a time. This shall soothe your tensions and help you think calmly about the problem at hand when you return to it after a few minutes.

5. Make sure you collect as much information as you can about the unfortunate situation you feel stuck in so that you can address it properly. If you have a web design project due in two days, and you are experiencing a bad creativity block, use the internet to brainstorm for ideas. You could check out ideas on Pinterest, talk to friends working in that field, or prepare a detailed questionnaire for your client so that you can extract as much information as you can from him/her. We normally fret during a difficult situation because we perceive it as trouble and because we do not have much information about how to tackle it. We address the problem using limited

information, a factor mostly governed by our fears and worries. This means we only see it from a negative lens. When we have enough information about a problem, we start seeing it from different angles. When our horizons broaden, our approach to perceive and tackle the problem changes too. This helps us better address the issue and eventually resolve it.

No matter what problem you may be facing, use this approach to embrace it. You will be surprised at how well you will manage it and how easily you pull yourself out of any messy situation.

#7: You are not process-oriented

Another weakness often displayed by mentally weak people is that of not being process oriented. A process-oriented person is someone who takes an interest in the process that leads to an outcome.

"Be goal-oriented," which simplified means to keep your eyes on the goal and to strive to achieve it, is very common advice. While this is an effective way to remain motivated, in addition to it, you need to focus on every little step of the process that paves your way towards the end goal; you need to become process-oriented too.

In our pursuit of a certain goal, we often encounter countless obstacles, many of which are scary enough to sabotage our confidence. What happens in such instances is that it strips us of our motivation and drive to move forward, which leads us to quit our goal.

If we are process-oriented, we perceive every situation, every turn, every obstacle, and every step we take as a part of the process. We do not treat it as an individual trouble, but as a component of the process that will transform us from a warrior into a survivor and then into a victorious champion.

To ensure we do not lose sight of our goals, we need to change our attitude towards the routine experiences and the unforeseen, undesirable events. This is what we refer to as being process-oriented and is oftentimes the best way to battle your obstacles. If you wish to be mentally tough and have a strong mentality that leads you to have several accolades to your name, you need to become process oriented. Let us see how you can do that.

How to Overcome this Problem

Make the commitment to start gradually working on the following guidelines so that you enduringly become more involved in the day-to-day activities that contribute towards your success.

1. Go through your weekly and daily To-do lists and use this review to analyze how every task leads you to the end goal.

2. Spend some time analyzing its importance and contribution towards the goal, so you adopt a healthier attitude towards it. You may be dreading going to a meeting with some potential investors, but when you think about how that may get you the funding you need for your business idea, you will feel more compelled to attend it.

3. Think of all the contingencies you are likely to experience along the way. Imagine the worst-case scenarios that can happen and then think of how they can make it difficult for you to move forward.

4. Think of how you can possibly tackle every problem. If there are problems that upset you, there are solutions you can implement as well. No matter how tough a problem appears, it always comes with a solution. For

instance, you may think there is no way out of a lawsuit you have been dragged into, but if you are not at fault, you will find a way out because there is always a way out of everything.

5. Perceive every problem as a little challenge you need to overcome to move on to the next step. Your goal is like the Candy Crush game. Every mission of every level of the game is like all the problems you experience along your journey. You need to surpass every level to move on to the next one just as you need to battle a problem to achieve your goal.

6. Be mindful of every problem and tackle it positively. Similarly, enjoy your accomplishments and celebrate every little milestone you achieve. This makes you feel prouder of yourself and refuels your motivation to move to the next step successfully.

No problem is too big, and no victory is too small. Just remember to have fun along the way and to feed your positivity so that even as you keep your eyes on the goal, the ball, you also cherish the memories you make along the way and use those as lessons on your path to the finish line. This empowers you, keeps you from giving in to defeat at the hands of fears, and helps you build a can-do attitude.

#8: You are not grateful or aware of your blessings

When was the last time you thought about any of your blessings? Have you stopped to be grateful for the laptop you own, the books you read, the ability to talk and move, the clothes you have, friends who support you in difficult times, the car you drive, the job you have, and the scores of other things that add value, convenience and comfort in your life every single day?

We often fail to take account of our blessings and pay gratitude for our blessings. This is especially true for all the people with a weak mindset. When you cannot achieve your goals, you feel insecure, and out of that, you somehow start blaming the world for your failures. Instead of trying to figure out why you cannot overcome your problems and take accountability for your situation, you feel the world owes you. If you ponder on the issue, you will realize that it stems from a lack of gratitude, as well.

If you are not grateful for your blessings, you simply lack the ability to be aware of your gifts. This makes you nurture a complaining attitude towards your life, an attitude that makes you not work towards your goal at all. A good antidote to this problem is to nurture gratitude.

How to Become More Grateful:

To become mentally stronger, focused, and optimistic, you need to nurture gratitude. Below are several strategies that will help you do this:

1. Upon waking up every morning, thank the universe or whatever force you believe in for giving you another day to move towards your goals. This instantly brightens up your mood and sets a positive tone for the day.

2. After every hour, identify any single blessing that is somehow contributing towards your goal and be thankful for it. You could be grateful for the coffee you just drank because it energized you to work for another hour. Be thankful for the HR management software you stumbled upon online because that helps you better organize your HR- related information.

3. Similarly, be grateful for everything (from small to big) that somehow benefits you and helps you nurture a positive attitude.

4. Simultaneously, be grateful for identifying and understanding your obstacles because they help you recognize your problems so that you tackle them on time and solve them effectively.

Doing this daily cheers you on and compels you to find appropriate solutions for your problems. Once you start doing this, it will help you make efficient use of your time, and instead of crying over spilled milk, you shall use that time to overcome hurdles.

#9: You do not improve your weaknesses and skillset

At birth, none of us has a huge set of skills or all the virtues we need to win over obstacles.

All the accomplished people you know and see and all the people you hear receiving praise for their achievements have not had it easy. To be this polished, refined version of themselves, they have worked on themselves over many years.

When you dream about your goals but somehow fail to put in the effort required to actualize them, you have the potential to be a champion, but sadly, you are not investing enough time, effort, and energy into the process. Your weak mentality keeps you from working on improving your shortcomings and diversifying your skillset. Therefore, you feel incompetent to tackle a certain goal.

When adversity attacks you, you feel you cannot handle it because you lack the right skills and tools. You often think, "if only I had the right skill or talent to address the situation better, I would have battled it nicely."

How to Overcome this Problem:

First, understand that no problem is bigger than your strength and might. Even if you possess all the amazing skills in the world, you cannot overcome a problem if you believe you are inadequate to defeat it. Now that you know that, keep in mind, too, that having a good skillset makes it easier for you to manage problems.

To become better equipped to handle obstacles, do the following:

1. Create a list of your current weaknesses related to the skillset you think keeps you from moving forward, enjoying good opportunities, and achieving your goals faster.

2. Pick any one area you would like to work on first or one you feel you can improve with ease.

3. Look for strategies that help you improve that shortcoming. For instance, if you need to become an Excel expert to create amazing accounts of yourself for a certain task, take a short Excel course or view tutorials online.

4. Work on these strategies every day, so you do something meaningful daily to improve on yourself.

5. Analyze your performance before and after working on your weaknesses. Use the difference in improvement to feel good about yourself. Applaud your efforts and keep moving forward.

Mental toughness and the fulfillment of your goals will not happen overnight, and self-development does not work like magic. However, if you commit to building habits every day, you will soon create a compound effect and will become a more confident, self-reliant, grateful, positive, and mentally stronger version of yourself.

In addition to mental toughness, you also need to develop the ability to work well and calmly under pressure because this ability is what ensures that your obstacles do not get the better of you and that you achieve your targets.

In the next section of the guide, we shall discuss how to improve your ability to perform well under pressure.

Section 3

How to Perform Well Under Pressure and Deal with Setbacks Positively

BELIEVE what your heart tells you, not what others say.

purehappylife.com

Peter Marshall, a Scots-American teacher, once said,

"When we long for life without difficulties, remind us that oaks grow strong in contrary winds and diamonds are made under pressure."

Have you ever wondered how Kobe Bryant scored a whopping 81 points in just one NBA game? Have you ever thought of how Rory McIlroy bounced back from terribly choking at the 2011 Masters to finally emerging victorious at the US Open soon after? Martin Turner, an expert at sport and psychology, says the victory of these two individuals is courtesy of their mentality and attitude.

Our triumphs are more about our mental game than the physical struggle. Life is rarely about how skilled or talented we are or how well we are aware of the tactics related to a situation. Oftentimes, all you need to win over all obstacles is the right attitude and the ability to perform optimally under pressure. This is what mental toughness is about and what you will learn in this section.

What Does Performing Well Under Pressure Mean?

The number one character trait that separates good entrepreneurs from extraordinary ones, good athletes from exceptionally talented ones, and anyone who is good at something from anyone who is great at the area is a person's ability to stay put in high-pressure situations to beat the odds against them. The finest of skills lose their value if you cannot perform well when you need it the most: the time of nerve-wracking, nail-biting competition.

Any two people with a similar skillset and training can perform extremely differently when confronted with tensile situations. What sets apart the one who grabs a gold medal from the one who does not is just the former's capacity to push forward in high-pressure situations.

If you wish to become an industry leader, you need to build robust psychological skills that help you fulfill your true potential in difficult situations. To become a leader, you also need to stay calm in such situations so that you help others unleash and optimize their potential as well.

We all have the gift of a beautiful mind. However, only those who treasure it and use it as a valuable weapon can transform their threats into opportunities.

Our ability to stay poised under pressure directly relates to how we respond to stress. Our initial response to stress is usually a reaction. Reactions are impulsive and irrational. When we react, we unconsciously pay heed to the first alarming thought that pops up in our mind, especially when we rapidly evaluate a stressful situation.

For instance, if a client points out a mistake in your work, instead of accepting your shortcomings, you snap back at him/her. You fail to gain a chance to participate in the international wrestling team, and without thinking things through, you quit your goal altogether.

The instant you face a challenging, demanding, and potentially debilitating situation, your first go-to reaction to it is to flee the situation altogether. We refer to this response as the fight or flight response, aka *the stress response.* This response is a major reason why you often quit your goals instead of fighting the struggles that attack you. When this response is active, you enter the *threat state* and allow your threats to get the better of you.

All those who choose to respond to the struggle and fight it instead of fleeing it can battle the challenge. They enter the *challenge state.* Even in that category, there are those who cannot perform optimally and those who rise above the challenge. Those in the latter category usually perform well under pressure. They do not allow their stress and struggles to get the better of them, and because of it, these people are often the ones who emerge as industry leaders, gold medalists, Olympic champions, and the accomplished people we all draw inspiration from and speak about often.

Performing well under pressure is an art form. It encompasses your ability to stay put when adversity strikes. Your ability to keep your volatile emotions under check and to manage the different physiological reactions you experience, such as muscle tension, increased heart palpitations, and sweaty palms. It also encompasses not giving into the pressure and breaking the barrage of thoughts you experience so that you can focus on the problem afoot and think things through.

This is not easy because you experience countless physiological reactions within a fraction of a second. With every reaction comes a thought that triggers another reaction, and before you realize it, you become emotionally and physically drained.

In such an emotionally and physically traumatizing situation, it is naturally difficult to maintain your calm and opt for a logical and beneficial situation. Seeking comfort is one of our innate human needs, which is why the minute we confront adversity, we look for ways to flee it.

Fleeing a problem is easier when compared to enduring the high-pressure situation or finding a way out of the mess. This explains why most of us quit all our goals - even the ones associated with our ambitions. This is the reason why we have more failures than successes to our credit.

When we decide to endure the tough time, keep our emotions under control, and ensure our sanity stays intact, we can move past it and emerge triumphant in the end. This ability to perform gracefully under pressure comes with mental toughness.

Let us look at how you can attain this ability and become the master of your impulse emotions and reactions.

How to Perform Well Under Pressure and Deal with Setbacks

The ability to enter the challenge state reflects your positive mental approach to high tensile situations when your mental resources fulfill the demands of high-pressure situations.

Whenever the stress response is active, we go through a range of intense physiological responses such as dry mouth, muscle tension, profuse sweating, increased heartbeat, nausea, and the likes. These responses give us the energy and stamina to fight or flee the situation.

Unfortunately, we often trigger this response unconsciously whenever we perceive even the slightest of change in our everyday situation as debilitating. Our ancestors faced threats such as hungry lions, saber-tooth tigers, and crazy avalanches that would cause unimaginable destruction.

As opposed to this, the dangers of today are more psychological and diverse than before. Our saber-tooth tigers are addressing an audience of 200 people, finding high paying clients, managing several tasks at once, making sure you do not lose your million-dollar position in the business industry, and the likes.

The instant we face a tough situation, our breathing becomes rapid and shallow; this is normally the first trigger of the stress response. When our brain receives this signal, it sets off the fight or flight response, and before we realize it, we feel stressed out and ready to break under pressure.

Your mission in life from this moment is to learn how to remain calm under pressure. Only then will you be able to fix the problem without letting it cloud your ability to think rationally.

Here is what you can do to ensure that.

#1: Reframe the Traumatizing Situation

When you are in a high-pressure situation, it is crucial that you stay focused on the task and trouble at hand. If you are busy fretting over how you will perform, you will only waste your brainpower.

Ironically, one of the common ways to approach a tensile situation is to unconsciously remind yourself of the trouble and tell yourself things such as "don't fail" or "don't mess it up." Contrary to our expectations, such suggestions end up sabotaging our confidence and increasing our chances of failure. Years of research show that when you remind yourself not to do something, you are likely to end up doing just that unconsciously.

Due to constant reminders of how you will fail, you perceive a high-pressure situation as a make-or-break situation and allow it to control you. In such situations, it is important that you stay focused and on task so that you stay poised. A good way to do that is to reframe the situation and perceive it differently. Some situations carry great weight, but oftentimes, the daily things that exhaust us are not actual do-or-die situations.

You need to eliminate the threatening aspect from the situation and learn to perceive situations as an opportunity to prove your mettle instead of a threat. If you fear a situation, you will not perform to the best of your abilities.

That negative element associated with a situation saps away all your energy and positivity and makes a slightly difficult task appear like a mountain you must surmount. You need to modify the way you think about a situation so that you can better prepare yourself to address it.

Here are a few ways to do that.

• When adversity strikes you, do not see it as a do-or-die situation. Strip off the element of fear from the situation by replaying the event in your mind with some funny background music and focus more on the music and less on the actual movie playing in your mind.

• Do this a few times until you feel less negative about the overall trouble.

• Next, treat it as a routine situation. Write down about it in your journal beginning from the start until the end. Let your thoughts and words flow freely and write down whatever pops up in your mind.

• When you finish the above task, take out all the negative words from the description such as "mess," "failure," "doomed," "loss," etc. Eliminate anything that is just an adjective and that does not contribute anything meaningful to the overall story.

• Read the account again, and this time, eliminate more words and phrases. Stick to only the actual event, the lessons drawn from it, the outcome, and the effects of the outcome on your psyche.

• By now, you should have a few sentences remaining. Finally, omit the _how it affects you_ part and write down what remains again.

• Read it aloud and notice how the episode becomes less traumatic than you thought it was. This is the actual event, and everything else that you associated with it was just your feelings of the experience.

- Observe the lesson, the results, and your shortcomings, so you can improve on them. This helps you nurture an optimistic outlook towards the event and learn from it instead of allowing it to control you.

#2: Predict and Plan for Crunch Times

You fail to perform calmly and rationally during crunch times because you are not aware of yourself and your work. Naturally, when you are not fully aware of who you are, how you work, what affects you, how your business functions, its internal and external environment, its strengths and weaknesses, and the likes, you will not be able to predict the unforeseen threats on time as well.

To keep your calm during high-pressure situations, it is important that you have a contingency plan for threatening situations ready beforehand. This way, every time adversity strikes you, you will have a few plans detailing how to tackle it. If plan A fails, you will have a spare plan B, and then maybe a plan C. There occasionally comes a time when all your plans fail, but if you have a habit of preparing for struggles in advance, you will not lose your motivation in such an instance.

1. To predict and plan for all crunch times, first examine yourself in detail. List down your weaknesses so that you can identify ways to tackle them on time; if procrastination is your weakness, maybe set great incentives on the fulfillment of your milestones.

2. Next, carry out an in-depth analysis of your work, business, or whatever you are trying to do. Figure out the possible threats associated with the external environment so you can better prepare a contingency plan.

3. Detail out the strengths and weaknesses of your work, skills, and business so you can better employ the strengths to tackle the weaknesses.

4. In addition, figure out all the areas you can outsource help from to ensure their smooth functioning during crunch times. For instance, if you are organizing a digital marketing workshop two weeks from now and you know taking care of the house and kids on that day will be difficult, get a house help or arrange for a babysitter for that day. This way, you will not mess up things on that day.

5. Prepare at least three plans for every contingency you fear will attack you. This ensures you have a few ideas ready and that you can use to combat an upsetting problem.

When misfortune knocks on your door, your first reaction is likely to be that of panic. Be aware of the physiological signs of panic, such as rapid heartbeat muscle tension, and starting to breathe quickly.

Every emotional state we experience stays for a maximum of 12 minutes; it lingers on only when we hold on to the respective thoughts. If you keep seething in anger, you will continue feeling angry. Now that you know that, if you choose to let go of the anger and focus more on what you can do, you will relieve yourself of that stress. Breathe, relax, and when you feel better, take out your contingency plans and act on them.

#3:   Have your prioritization strategy at the ready

Not every hardship you experience deserves your time and attention. At times, you will have tasks that seem to be high priority, but when you assess their importance, you realize they are not as significant for you as you believed them to be in the first place.

When you prepare your To-do list and contingency plan, assess the importance of every task for you, and examine its relevance to your end goal. If a task is low priority, there is likely to be an emergency attached to it and will be of low priority too. Delegate that responsibility to someone right now and inform them of any contingencies that you assume to come their way. This way, you relieve yourself of undue pressure and can focus better on your actual, high priority tasks. Judi Rhee Alloway, a Life Coach working at the Imagine Leadership LLC, strongly believes in this approach to handling crunch times.

Similarly, when a misfortune attacks you unexpectedly, reflect on its significance in your life. If it is something you can avoid, immediately say no. Not every trouble deserves your attention. For instance, if you are already getting late for a business meeting and you get a call from a friend saying how he is coming to see you in five minutes, politely refuse him because you are already on your way out. Call and meet the friend later, but for now, focus on what matters: your important business meeting.

#4: Be mindful of the Present Moment

The minute a hardship comes your way, you are likely to ruminate on all the different things you did wrong to invite that misfortune your way. You are likely to criticize yourself, blame others for misguiding you, lament on how you opted for the wrong choices, and continuously worry about everything *that has happened.*

While it is natural to behave that way, you should understand that this habit is what fuels your weak mindset and keeps you from toughening yourself up so that you can perform well under pressure.

It is easier to battle a misfortune if you are mindful of the present. The minute you give in to negative thinking about your past or to how things will not shape up well for you in the future, remind yourself of the situation that demands your attention. Take a deep breath and realign your focus on the situation at hand. Do that a few times, and you will concentrate better on the problem.

#5: Break the Problem into Smaller Parts

Every big project is likely to overwhelm you, be it a regular project or one that has just landed on your plate unexpectedly. Naturally, the latter will upset you more because it is huge, and secondly, it is completely uninvited.

That said, you cannot avoid your contingencies if you wish to progress towards your goal. To make your problem less overwhelming, do not look at it as a whole. Instead, break it down into smaller, more manageable tasks. According to Laura DeCarlo of Career Directors International, this strategy works well at helping you stay calm under pressure.

If you have an unexpected project to complete in a day, chop it down into smaller milestones such as gathering resources for it, assigning tasks, working on the tasks, etc. When your big task breaks down into smaller milestones, it becomes easier to meet your goals and tackle the problem in a systematic manner.

#6: Think of What You Can Do Right Now

According to Judi Rhee Alloway from the Imagine Leadership LLC, one great way to avoid crunch times and battle them nicely is to think of what you can do right now.

There is always something you can do right now to clear the mess a little bit; every time the stakes are high, ask yourself, "What can I do right now?" Write down the answers and pick out any one task you can do and complete as soon as possible.

Whatever task you decide to work on, do it right away without overthinking it. The more you think about a task, the deeper you are likely to get into analysis paralysis, which we can define as the inability to take any action at all. Analysis paralysis is a major reason why you give in to your negative thoughts during high-pressure situations and why you do not take any meaningful action. Break this cycle of negativity by getting straight to business and doing even something very little to make some improvement.

#7:   Use the Eisenhower model

The Eisenhower Model states that we always have four types of tasks:

1. **Urgent and Important Tasks:** These are all the tasks that need your attention urgently and are highly important to the accomplishment of your goal. You need to engage in these tasks as soon as possible to skyrocket your productivity. If you have recently started a social media marketing agency, your urgent and high priority task would be to have a solid presence online, particularly on social media.

2. **Important, but Not Urgent Tasks:** These tasks are quite significant in nature and relate to your goal too, but they are not too urgent to execute. You can carry them out on a later date without losing any productivity. For example, to run your social media marketing agency successfully, you need to consider collaborating with already established marketing agencies. This task is

important and can boost your outcome but is not necessarily crucial right now.

3. **Urgent, but Not Important Tasks:** These are all the tasks that require your urgent attention but are not too significant in nature, particularly in relation to your goal. For example, you may need to pick up your suit from the dry cleaner right now so that you can have something to wear as you attend a seminar tomorrow. This is an urgent task, but not a very important one, especially if you have other things to wear to the seminar.

4. **Neither Important Nor Urgent Tasks:** These tasks are neither urgent nor too crucial for you to carry out right away. For instance, doing the laundry right now is neither important nor urgent and does not relate to your first weekly target, which may be to register your company's name.

Elva Bankins Baxter, who works at a high executive position at Bankins Consulting, Inc., advocates for the use of the Eisenhower Model to identify your urgent, important, unimportant, and not-so-urgent tasks.

Every time you sit to work, analyze all your tasks lined up for the week, and then divide them into the four categories discussed above. The ones in the first category demand your serious and utmost attention. Once you figure them out, work on them right away, followed by those in the second matrix. You then need to work on the tasks in the third category and then finally cater to the fourth category.

When you are 100% aware of the tasks that need your time, effort, and attention, you ease off the pressure and easily commit to working on only the most pressing tasks.

#8: Review Your Previous Pressure Points and Figure out Your Patterns

Time is a very expensive commodity. Once it passes, you cannot get it back. While you cannot get back your lost time or go back in time to do what you wanted to do, you can learn to manage it efficiently. Learning from your mistakes so that you do not repeat them is a great way to manage your time better and improve your productivity.

Review your performance on different tasks repeatedly so that you can better understand your pressure points. This helps you identify your different behavioral patterns so that you know exactly when you lose your calm and give into the high-pressure situations.

Once you have that knowledge, create a prevention strategy that helps you keep from repeating your mistakes. This plan helps you mitigate the huge amount of unexpected risks associated with challenges and additionally helps you minimize stress. Tameka Williamson, a renowned consultant working at the Celestial & Associates Consulting, vouches for this strategy and often uses it to save herself from experiencing hassle and crunch times.

#9: Separate the External and Internal Pressures

Pressure adds in a lot of urgency into the completion of your tasks. Oftentimes, this urgency comes from mixing up external and internal pressures. Tmima Grinvald, the founder of the successful business consulting firm, The Round Well, believes that it is imperative to understand your internal and external pressures in every difficult situation so you can discern between both and focus only on the external ones.

Every time you feel stuck in a rut, analyze the external pressure, and keep your sight only on that. Separate your internal stress, tensions, and agony from the outward pressure by concentrating on the problem at hand. Take deep breaths, think of your end goal, and imagine yourself achieving it. Once you can clearly see that picture, ask yourself *what you really want to do.*

Use that positivity to assess the actual problem and you will start finding it easier to create solutions to resolve it. Once you focus more on the external pressure, use it as an opportunity to grow bigger and better.

According to Anjali Chugh, a successful business advisory firm, you need to push back at your pressure to allow your energy to expand. Every crunch time comes with a unique opportunity to grow better and prove your worth. Just use all the strategies discussed previously and your inner urge to prove your mettle to work well under pressure and allow your horizons to broaden.

#10: Sleep well

In her popular book, <u>The Sleep Revolution</u>, Ariana Huffington talks about the importance of sleeping well daily so that you can feel healthy and be able to tackle all your routine tasks as well as the crunch times like a pro. If your body and mind lack proper rest, you cannot think and act optimally. This explains why you feel lethargic day in and day out, and why you quickly give into challenges that threaten to derail you from the path to your goals.

Get back at your troubles like a fierce tiger by refueling your energy first. Build a healthy sleep routine by setting a fixed sleep and wake-up time. Go to bed at least 30 minutes prior to your bedtime and do something soothing, such as reading a good book or listening to light, relaxing music. Keep your phone away, as the blue rays emitted by the screens disrupt your circadian rhythm, which keeps you from sleeping on time and well.

Stick to this routine for three weeks, and you will build a healthy sleep cycle soon. If you stick to this, you will immediately notice a massive, positive improvement in your cognition, stamina, focus, attention, and ability to manage stress. This will help you stay positive, fresh, and invigorated round the clock but especially during tough times, which will help you execute tasks on time.

Alexandra Salamis of Integral Leadership Design, a business and leadership consultancy firm that helps leaders conquer challenges to achieve and skyrocket business growth, strongly advocates for the power of a good night's rest and advises anyone who wishes to achieve his or her goals to sleep on time.

#11: Have a Routine and Stick to It

All experts believe in the divine objectivity associated with the routine of things. If you examine the routine of athletes who train for the Olympics, or the routines of young associates trying to become top-notch lawyers, you will note that they adhere strictly to their daily practices, and by diligently obliging to these tough routines, they eventually cross the finish line.

Rachel Lourdes Mestre, a successful life coach and owner of the Rachel Mestre LLC, a renowned management consulting company that specializes in offering crisis management and value enhancement services for businesses, believes that it is crucial for everyone to develop a healthy and active work routine, and to stick to it diligently no matter what. Having a routine helps you build a strong character that helps you home in on your project's scope with dedication and clarity, and never surrender to pressures.

It takes time to incorporate all these hacks into your routine. It is, therefore, best to implement one strategy at a time and slowly pack all these guidelines into your daily routine.

It is crucial to turn these practices into habits so that you can gradually improve your mental toughness and the ability to handle high-pressure situations like a pro.

Now let us move on to the next section, where we shall discuss the 40% rule of mental toughness that will give you more clarity on how to unlock your true potential and actualize it.

Section 4

The 40% Rule of Mental Toughness

" Have enough courage to trust
love one more time and
always one more time "

**epic
quotes**

There is an overabundance of business, success, and growth-related books in the market, and while you will find numerous growth hacks in them, not many will talk about the *40% rule of mental toughness.*

If you wish to be the true champion in your real life, and if you want to actualize every high priority goal, you need to abide by this golden rule. Since we know you have that spark inside you, YOU also need to learn how to use and implement this golden rule of success so that you can tap and unleash that potential within you.

What is the 40% Rule of Mental Toughness?

In his bestselling book, Living with a SEAL, Jesse Itzler talks about the valuable life lessons he learned from living with a SEAL. The first time Itzler met the SEAL (whose real name is David Goggins), he was running a striking 100-mile-run, and he did a great job at it while Itzler struggled to run on the track. He implored Goggins to live with him and his family for a month, and during that time, he found out the amazing 40% rule of mental toughness that slowly helped Itzler become the mastermind of his life.

According to the 40% rule, most of us work at our 40% optimal level. We feel we are giving our work our best shot and pushing ourselves hard to get everything done. Even with the toughest of routines, many of us are only functioning at a 40% level. We have the capacity to do so much more. We even know we can take on more challenges and really go the extra mile. Nonetheless, we fall short of doing that because we apply our brakes the minute we reach our 40% level.

Our 40% working capacity is like the pit stop where we rest every day, plan to move past it the next day, but one way or another find ourselves taking a hiatus at exactly that point for days to come. This happens because every time we try to push ourselves harder to extend our limit, our mind tells us how we cannot move even an inch further. We feel exhausted, mentally drained, and incapable of doing anything else. We feel we have given it our 100% best, but we *are only at the 40% level.*

The truth is many of us give up right when it starts to suck. Have you ever felt your muscles becoming excruciatingly sore while working out? If your answer is no, it is because you never pushed yourself to do another rep of push-ups or another set of burpees just when you felt your muscles getting a wee bit sore. This is how most of us function. This is also the reason why majority of us only yearn for success but never actualize our dreams or goals.

Whether you want to build a million-dollar company, lose 30 pounds, master the art of meditation and really control your subconscious mind, position yourself as the best motivational speaker to date, give up on alcohol and build a healthy lifestyle, or do anything you truly feel connected to, you must unlock your 100% potential and fulfill it.

You must go the extra mile. You must move past the 40% mark and push yourself harder and forward. Unless you push yourself harder, you will never realize your full potential. Yes, you will struggle all this while, but with every push, you will become aware of your capacity to work even harder.

Continuing with the example of Goggins, Goggins asked Itzler to do a few pull-ups. Itzler did about eight. Goggins asked him to take a 30-second break and go for another round. Itzler struggled with doing more pull-ups but managed to do about four more. Goggins then asked him to do it another time and pushed Itzler to keep doing more pull-ups spaced with 30-second breaks.

Every time Itzler felt he could not do a single more pull-up, Goggins encouraged him to take another one and then another one. Goggins showed Itzler that if we try to push ourselves forward, we can really cross the limit we set for ourselves and go a step further every time.

David Goggins holds the World Record for doing the most pull-ups, 4030 in 24 hours, and is a fifth-place finisher at the Badwater 135, a famous 135-mile race held in the Death Valley.

The startling fact is not that Goggins did all of that, the startling fact is that he did all that while suffering from atrial septum defect, a heart condition where one has a hole in the walls of the heart, a condition that limits endurance and stamina. Goggins must have gone through hell while pushing his limits, but he knew that the hole in his heart was not big enough to stop him from becoming the champion of his life. He knew his strength was stronger and fiercer than that hole, and he worked hard to prove himself right.

What Goggins proved to Itzler that stimulated him to do was to push beyond his limit and go past the 40% mark. He showed him that we have a lot more potential than we give ourselves credit for.

We never really tap into our full potential, which is why we do not realize, explore, and unleash it. If we do not surrender to our internal pressures, keep hammering ourselves to go the extra mile, and really push ourselves to go for another round, we can unlock our true potential and use it to objectify all our goals. The story of Itzler and Goggin is not a mere theory. Scientific findings have proven the same.

A study conducted in 2008 concluded that to achieve your goals and unlock your maximum potential, you need to believe in yourself; the study divided participants into two groups. One group received a placebo and told it was caffeine, while the other received actual caffeine. The goal was to help them lose weight.

The results showed that those on a placebo lost more weight compared to those on caffeine. This study reaffirmed the fact that we have great potential, and our limits are a result of our limiting beliefs. We need to understand that if we are to revise our limits so that nothing really stops us. What we believe to be impossible is often just a glitch in our minds and the 40% rule doing its rounds.

We do not know our limits because we have hardly ever pushed ourselves very hard to reach them. Because of this, many of us feel we lack the capacity to take on different goals or achieve that one difficult goal we have been trying to accomplish for years.

We can do it, but to do it, we need to push ourselves past the 40% limit. Here are some hacks to help you do that.

How to Move Past the 40% Limit

Winston Churchill once rightfully said, *"Success is stumbling from failure to failure with no loss of enthusiasm."*

This a very appropriate definition of what you need to do to achieve every goal you have ever set. Whether you wish to become a successful entrepreneur, land that million-dollar job, or become a gold medalist, you need to have the strength to endure failures and treat them as opportunities and as steppingstones towards success.

In addition, you need to have a knack to push yourself forward and harder after enduring every setback so that you work even harder and achieve your goal this time around. This cannot happen unless you stop giving into the 40% rule. Here are a few strategies that should help you learn to push past the 40% rule.

#1: Exhaust Your Limit

You will never realize your maximum potential unless you fully exhaust yourself. This does not mean you should work round the clock, but this does mean that you need to work harder during your work hours. If you feel you have worked for five hours on a task and it is enough to give you a good result, look for another way in the sixth hour that could really skyrocket your success. If you have done 50 push-ups with burpees, try five more. If you had a tough 8-hour workday and you now feel that you cannot work out for 30 minutes at all, *do it anyway.*

To truly understand and explore your limit, you need to exhaust yourself fully. This may sound harsh, but ask yourself this one question, "When does success come easily?" It never does, and it never will!

You are a warrior. The amazing life you have always wanted is yours for the taking. However, you can only be the BEST, most amazing version of yourself if you push yourself forward and really sweat it out. Do not stop pushing yourself until you feel soreness from within. That is when you should stop for a little while, rest, and repeat the cycle.

#2: Move a Step Further

When you feel your muscles sore and tender, and really feel you cannot move another inch, push yourself forward to do one more difficult task. If you have done 60 mountain climbers and that has been your best to-date, try three more, take a short break of 20 seconds, and try five more. If you have knocked the doors of five potential clients but are yet to get any investor onboard yet, knock the sixth door.

You need to adopt the principle of moving a step further every time you try your hand at achieving a certain target. Just achieving your previous target should not be your goal. You need to do even better the next day and then the next day. If you keep pushing yourself forward, you will only become wiser, smarter, and tougher. You can do it - and you will. Just trust yourself.

#3: Do not Listen to Your Limiting Beliefs

We have elaborated on how a weak mindset contributes towards your inability to take on challenges and achieve your goals. A weak mindset comprises of toxicity and limiting beliefs. These are all the beliefs that remind you of your failures and strengthen your faith in the unhealthy belief that your potential can never grow. The truth is that we are all capable of achieving growth and success if we try.

The number one reason you give in to your weaknesses is not that you are inadequate, but because you listen to your limiting beliefs. Every time you face a roadblock, you make a U-turn and go back to the start. You change your goal altogether or settle on the belief that you can never do anything right. Both attitudes are unhealthy and are a great explanation for why you are struggling to stand straight while your peers are accomplishing one feat after another.

Tune into your thoughts every time you try to go the extra mile, work harder, or take one activity on your plate. If you hear things such as, "You cannot do this," "You don't have the potential to achieve the target," "You will fall short of doing it like before," or "there is already so much to take care of," acknowledge that annoying voice and accept it as your inner critic spewing venom at you. While you should acknowledge it, you should not pay heed to it. Immediately after hearing this voice, find a positive replacement for it and practice it repeatedly. You need to drill that new, positive suggestion in your subconscious constantly so that your subconscious mind accepts it.

The reason why you believe the limiting belief is that you have hammered it into your subconscious mind over the years by constantly reminding yourself of your fears, setbacks, and lack of potential. You need to change that internal program by rewiring your mind to think positively. This can happen if you remind yourself of your strengths, talents, amazing potential, and drill relevant positive suggestions into your subconscious mind repeatedly.

Greatness always comes with enduring pain and suffering, and it is not all that bad either. You think you cannot do it, but you can. Just trust yourself, believe in the positive affirmation you are chanting, and visualize yourself achieving that tough target. You will feel amazed at how strong you are and the many brilliant things you discover you can do if you keep pushing yourself forward.

#4: Face Your Fears

Nobody has ever been able to make it to the finish line without embracing fears. Like setbacks, fears are just tiny glitches that ought to help us grow. When we surrender to our fears, we let them grow bigger. To break your inner shackles and move past the 40% limit, you need to become empowered. For that, you will have to face your fears.

List your fears and elaborate on how they make you feel. For instance, your fear could be collapsing while working out for an hour; or you may fear not being able to make it to the top 5 contestants in the music show you have been selected in, or your fear may be to lose a grant you have worked at for five years.

Whatever your fear is, describe it and then remind yourself of how you will not make it to the final step if you do not have the courage to embrace this fear now. Many before you have done that and many after you will do it. You will stay here, cribbing about your pain if you do not try to move forward.

You know you can do it. You have made it so far, and if you keep going, it is only a matter of time before you hug your goal hard and tight. You just need to go a little further and believe that you can do it. Do not allow your fears to get the better of you; be ready to embrace them and to challenge them.

#5: Become physically stronger

Physical fitness has a direct relation to mental toughness. If you can work out for an hour without giving up, you can easily engage in tasks that require mental effort for hours too. Physical fitness instills stamina, confidence, and grit. It teaches you about sticking to your goals, pushing yourself harder, and going the extra mile even when the going gets tough.

To implement the 40% rule of mental toughness in your life so that you can uncover your genuine potential and abilities, incorporate physical activities in your life and build a habit of exercising at least six days a week - if not daily.

Find any rigorous physical activity you enjoy doing, such as swimming, aerobics, Pilates, or even a sport that makes your muscles work out and engage in it every day for at least 60 minutes. Doing that straight away is hard, which is why you need to start small. Begin with 10 to 15 minutes of workout and slowly build your way up. Once you can comfortably exercise for 15 minutes for a month, take it up to 20 minutes and then 25 and so on until you can work out for 60 minutes daily.

Once you settle into that routine, focus on increasing your energy and intensity level. You may think you have exhausted your limit in the 40 to 60 minutes of workout, but if you closely examine your performance, you will realize that you are only performing to your 3o% or a maximum level of 50%. If you are doing jumping jacks, you may not be doing with 100% intensity. If you are transitioning from downward facing dog to cobra pose repeatedly, you may not be flexing your muscles enough.

Whatever workout you are doing, engage in it with more energy and enthusiasm. Push your body harder, stretch your muscles more, try one more rep, and do it with more effort. Believe you can do it and push yourself forward. You will be surprised at the amazing capability and potential you have.

Ensure to do this daily and keep track of your performance. Write down about the duration of your workout, intensity level, weakness you showed, milestones you achieved, and so on daily, and review your performance at the end of the day. In just a week, you will observe a massive difference and improvement in your stamina and endurance levels, which will show that you *can do a lot more if only you try.*

#6: Review and Improve

As you slowly build your tendency and ability to work harder and take on more challenges, review your performance over the course of a couple of weeks, identify your weaknesses, and improve yourself. If you have not worked on a task on time for a couple of days, start doing that more now.

Moreover, figure out your peak energy time and keep your important tasks for that time duration. Your peak energy time is that window of the day when you feel the most active and energetic. During this window, you are ready to tackle big challenges and can move past even the toughest of roadblocks. Observe your performance in different activities over a period of two to four weeks so that you can understand your peak energy time better.

Once you figure that out, schedule your important tasks for that time of the day, and push yourself harder during that time. The great thing is that pushing harder is easier than it seems. You only need to push yourself harder for a few days; soon after, you will get the hang of working on a strict schedule like a pro.

Another aspect of mental toughness is to build your emotional intelligence and consistently work on growing it. This directly associates with your ability to work harder and grow forward. The next section looks at how you can do that.

Section 5

Emotional Strength, Sense of Purpose, and Direction

THERE IS NOTHING LIKE RETURNING TO A PLACE THAT REMAINS UNCHANGED TO FIND THE WAYS IN WHICH YOU YOURSELF HAVE ALTERED.
- NELSON MANDELA

planeta.wikispaces.com/nelsonmandela#quotes

If you have ever read Nelson Mandela's life history and struggles, you will know that goals do not come easy. Additionally, you would have also noticed that Mandela was able to achieve his targets by working hard and by being emotionally strong. He was quite emotionally strong and calm as well, and his emotional intelligence played a massive role in determining his success.

He was also clear about what he wanted to achieve in life and made sure to strive towards that goal every day. His mission was always to emancipate Black people across the globe, and primarily in South Africa, from all the suffering inflicted on them. The Black community in South Africa owes its freedom and the right to live freely to Mandela's efforts. Had he not been clear about what he wanted or lacked a vivid sense of purpose in his life, he would not have achieved the stature he is revered and remembered for now.

To find the right direction in your life and the courage to follow it to the very end, you need clarity. Unless you can see a clear picture of what you want in your head, you will always move haphazardly in gazillion directions often to find yourself at point zero repeatedly.

For Mandela, his goal and purpose were always clear. He was fully aware of and settled on his life's vision, which is why he kept moving forward with perseverance and resilience. He surely encountered many roadblocks and battled countless struggles, but he never succumbed to the pressures because he knew what he wanted and had compelling reasons to follow through with that goal.

In this section of the guide, we shall look at how you can build your emotional strength and find a clear purpose in life.

How Emotional Strength Affects Your Success

Emotional strength aka emotional intelligence (EI) or emotional quotient (EQ) refers to your ability to keep your emotions in check, to manage the intense ones, and to use that awareness to adopt the right thought patterns, attitude, and behavior at the right time.

Emotional strength also encompasses the ability to comprehend the emotions of others and manage them effectively so that you can keep situations calm and peaceful.

If you are wondering about the influence this has on your ability to remain mentally strong and to achieve your goals, here is how:

1. Every time you go through a bout of anger or a volatile episode of jealousy, how do you behave? You are likely to act irrationally, make hasty decisions, make mountains out of molehills, and then later whine about how you did not think things through. Sadly, this is how many of us behave because we lack the emotional strength and calmness to keep our emotions in check, to control them instead of them controlling us. This would not be the case if you observed and analyzed your emotions and calmed yourself down before your volatile emotions compelled you to make a wrong decision. When you are emotionally strong, you take calculated, informed steps and soothe your stressed nerves to ensure you move seamlessly towards your end goal.

2. Secondly, a lack of emotional awareness and strength keeps you from sticking to your goal for long. Every time adversity strikes you, you have second thoughts about your mission and, oftentimes, end up quitting it altogether. You wish to persevere like Colonel Sanders did until he eventually created his chain of billion-dollar restaurants (KFC) at the age of 85, but somehow you end up surrendering to your anger, frustration, envy, fears, and apprehensions every time. This will not be the case if you keep a leash on your emotions and if you observe them so that you comprehend them better and then assuage your worries without giving into them. If you work on developing emotional strength, you too can be the Colonel Sanders of your life and that too at any age.

3. If you are emotionally strong, you become better aware of your highs and lows and make good use of this information. When you are too excited, you are likely to celebrate your success more and not work at all for days to come; you are also likely to forget working hard amidst that enthusiasm or even turn into a swollen head and underestimate your challenges. As opposed to this, if you feel extremely depressed, you are likely to nurture irrational fears, create self-doubt, procrastinate working on your goal, and never take any meaningful action. Both states are worrisome and only lead to a disastrous situation. You can easily avoid these instances if you become emotionally intelligent. You will become better aware of your emotional triggers, understand your mood swings and depression phases, and know exactly when you feel too ecstatic to think clearly. You will find the right strategies you can use to manage your emotions on time to avoid procrastination and your tendency to turn into a Mr./Ms. Know-it-all who only knows - but never acts.

4. Emotional strength also comes in handy while managing and leading people. You want to be more than good at what you do; you want to be the best! That comes with the ability to lead people because no matter what you do, you must work with some people, which also comes with the task of influencing and persuading people to do what you want. If you are emotionally strong, you can use your poise and charisma to influence others and stay calm when others behave irrationally. This draws people towards you and turns you into an inspiration.

As you can see, being emotionally strong has many advantages. Now let us discuss some hacks on how to attain this virtue.

How to Develop Emotionally Resiliency

To become emotionally stronger, employ the following strategies:

#1: Take Stock of Your Five Sense to Re-Focus

In the heat of intense, emotional moments, it is easy for your emotions to sweep you away. If the emotion is seemingly positive, the feeling is great and warms you up, but if the emotion is one of sadness, anger, or anything you perceive as negative, it upsets you and is likely to spiral out of control.

When you experience an emotion you perceive as negative, you need to take an immediate break from whatever you are going through and realign your focus on your five senses. This makes you more mindful of the present moment, shifts your focus from the worries to here and now, and helps you keep your anger or anxiety from storming out of your reach.

Here is what you should do:

1. Take stock of how you feel and note down your feelings. Write down your feelings as you feel them (freestyle it) without attaching any sort of judgment or label. If you are angry, put it down as "anger." If you feel envy rising inside you, jot that down. This acknowledgment alone is enough to validate your emotions and calm them down.

2. Consider your body's reactions to those feelings without judging them too. If your anxiety makes your skin feel hot or heartbeat incredibly fast, notice and

acknowledge that. Write that down and only observe without letting these realizations upset you.

3. Elaborate on how the emotion makes you feel and listen to it. If you can feel anger stirring inside you, what does it have to say? If you are anxious, why is that? How does that make you feel? Doing this helps you better understand the reason behind an intense emotion and gives you cues on how to soothe them.

4. Observe how each emotion feels and tastes, the sounds and noises it creates inside you, and the shape it takes inside you. For instance, if its anger, it is likely to feel like a fire burning inside you that is likely to taste hot, gurgle, and bubble hard inside you, smell pungent, and take the shape of a fiery storm inside you. If it is envy, it may have a purple or dark green color, look like a small, poisonous seed that is slowly growing bigger and creating sharp sounds inside you. Engage your five senses in the experience by assigning different features to your emotion. This animates the emotion and takes out the element of fear from it.

5. In a matter of minutes, you will feel more settled into the present moment and shall be able to manage your volatile emotions better.

You need to apply this practice for some time. Once you feel you have a better grasp on your emotions, dig deeper into understanding them. Meditation helps you with this trick nicely.

#2: Meditate to Gain Awareness of Your Emotions

Emotional awareness is crucial to acquiring the emotional strength and resilience you need to leash your rage, jealousy, and other intense emotions. You also require it to keep your anxiety and depression from exacerbating, so you never lose sight of your goals. Meditating regularly helps you inculcate, sustain, and build this ability.

Meditation is a beautiful practice that calms your racing mind and helps you take stock of your thoughts and emotions by shifting your focus from everything else to the present moment. You feel chaotic and troubled because of the barrage of thoughts always upsetting you.

When you stop worrying about everything all at once, relax, and take one thing at a time, you understand your emotions. When you know what every emotion means and its root cause, you resolve the matter accordingly and use appropriate strategies to tackle it.

Here is a simple meditative practice that will help you gain awareness of your emotions.

1. After you have practiced the exercise discussed above, you are likely to feel calmer.

2. When your calmness settles, pick an emotion you would like to observe and understand. Pick only one emotion at a time and separate other emotions from the one you want to reflect on. For instance, if you feel hurt, scared, and angry about a certain instance, think of the strongest or most predominant emotion of the lot, pick it, and reflect on it first. Every emotion has a different meaning; oftentimes, one emotion produces scores of other emotions and therefore, if you figure out the dominant one and understand it, you are likely to fix the other emotions as well.

3. Once you have selected an emotion, ask yourself why you feel that way. Play the "why game" for a while and ask yourself why you feel a certain way on every answer until you dig into it as far as you can go. For example, if

you ask yourself, "Why I feel depressed or dejected or angry?" and you get the answer "Because I lost a client" or any other reason, ask yourself why that happened. Keep probing into the matter until you reach a conclusion. For instance, you may realize that the root cause of your anger over not getting a scholarship is because you did not work hard enough for it.

4. When you have clearer answers to your emotional issues and have somewhat identified the root causes for your intense emotions, think of the different strategies you can use to mitigate the problem. If you are not happy with your performance, what can you do to improve it? If you fall short of achieving a certain milestone, maybe you need to change your strategy this time.

5. Once you have some ideas, turn them into action plans, and start working on them.

Use this approach to dig into the variety of intense and volatile emotions you repeatedly experience so that you can explore them better, comprehend, and acknowledge them. This also helps you become aware of the different factors that trigger your intense emotions and exacerbate them. If you know why you feel angry and what sets off your anger, you can avoid that situation beforehand.

#3: Accept Your Emotions Without Labeling Them

Emotions often exacerbate and cause you to make irrational decisions because you label them as bad and negative. Start accepting your emotions as they are without attaching any sort of ill sentiments or labels to them. If you are angry, accept your anger as it is. If you are sad, embrace your sadness. The more meaning and judgment you attach to an emotion, the bigger it grows.

On the other hand, when you let it be and accept it just as an emotion that will subside on its own if you do not hold on to it, the faster it will gradually die down. Allow your emotions to settle down on their own, which you can do by observing them without judging them. Doing this helps you stay calm amidst intense anger, anxiety, fear, jealousy, and rage, which helps you manage your emotions better.

#4: Do Not React Volatile Behavior Shown by Others

It is difficult to stay cool if others around you are erupting like a lava-emitting volcano. With that mentioned, such times are when you need to exhibit your emotional strength so that you can influence others positively. Whenever someone shows volatile behavior, excuse yourself from the situation if possible. If that is not an option, stay calm and quietly stand in one corner without reacting to any comment or gesture the person makes.

After the person calms down, talk to him/her assertively about the situation and give him/her your two cents on appropriate behavior and about responding to situations. Staying calm in such situations helps you come off as a poised, confident, and wise person who knows how to control dynamic situations.

Diligently working on these tips will help you build emotional resilience and inner strength that ensures you achieve your goals. This process also becomes easier when you have a clear sense of purpose in life.

How to Find Clear Direction in Life

M. Russell Ballard, an American religious leader and successful entrepreneur once said,

"Often, the lack of clear direction and goals can waste away our time and energy and contribute to imbalances in our lives. A life that gets out of balance is much like a car tire that is out of balance. It will make the operation of the car rough and unsafe. Tires in perfect balance can give a smooth and comfortable ride. So it is with life. The ride through mortality can be smoother for us when we strive to stay in balance."

This quote says everything about having a clear direction in life. It imparts meaning, empowerment, and value to your life because a life without a clear vision and direction does not get you anywhere.

We often complain about how we never complete anything worthwhile and how our life lacks structure. What we are unaware of is that this happens due to a lack of purpose in life.

Here is what you should do to organize your life by finding a clear purpose first.

#5: Find Your Core Values

Your core values are the principles and beliefs you abide by. For instance, if honesty is your core value, you will observe it in every aspect of your life. If you believe in empowerment for all, you will never snub anyone's right to think or act a certain way. To understand the vision and purpose of your life better, first detail out your core values.

Think of what you believe in as well as the values you never want to compromise on. List these down and elaborate on their significance in your life. Explain how each value adds meaning to your life and what you should do to follow it.

Go a step further and read up on different subjects to get more clarity on the things you believe in and expose yourself to more and new information that helps you understand your core values better.

#6: Find Out What Type of Player You Are

Gary Vaynerchuk, a social media and marketing expert, advises everyone to identify their true type after analyzing their core values. Gary and many other accomplished people across the globe strongly believe that not everyone is born to become an entrepreneur or a business tycoon. Some people perform best in jobs, running small businesses, or working at lower positions in an organization. This is nothing to be ashamed of or to feel bad about. We all have our strong suits and level of competence. It is best to figure out what you are most suited for so you can then devise your career pathway accordingly.

Conduct thorough self-audits on a regular basis so that you can continuously discover your strengths, weaknesses, core competencies, shortcomings, good virtues, accomplishments, skills, and talents. Write down what each of these means to you and the influence this meaning has on your life. Connect the dots by finding a nexus between your strengths, past accomplishments, things you have been doing professionally for years, talents, skills, etc.

For example, if you are good at marketing, have worked as a marketer for years and enjoy guiding people but are tired of your current marketing job, you could teach a course at an institute and then create marketing programs of your own to sell and earn a living.

If you figure out that you are better suited at some lower position, do not feel bad about it; accept it as a part of your personality. Give your job your 100%, and as you get better at it, you will enjoy it more and come across better growth opportunities.

#7: Try 90-Day Sprints

Peter Drucker, renowned business and management guru, planned his entire life in 18-month increments. Instead of planning his life five to ten years ahead of time, he would think of what he wanted 18 months from the current day and set goals accordingly. You can do the same. Think of what brings you value and meaning, and what things you cannot make do without and set compelling goals for 18 months from now.

Once you set a goal, create a plan of action for it by chopping it down into monthly and bi-monthly installments. Start implementing the plan, and once you actualize the milestone, take it forward from there. If your first goal for 18 months is to launch your own HR management software and make a thousand sales for it, your next goal could be to sell it internationally.

Once you achieve your 18-month targets, compare it with what you had planned, as well as what happened right or wrong during the process phase. This helps you get valuable feedback and bring positive improvements to your life.

#8: Review Your Goals Regularly to Identify Your Vision Better

It is not always easy or possible to identify your clear vision instantly. Finding a vision and purpose takes time. Give yourself time, so you get more clarity on your life's vision. To do that, review your goals regularly by revisiting them once every month. The more you explore your goal and ponder on your connection with it, the more cues you get about your true vision. Write down those cues and meditate on them so that you can identify your niche in the world.

Section 6

Overcome Your Fears and Anxiety; Move Outside of Your Comfort Zone

Fears and anxiety have a terrible habit of creeping up on you just when you are about ready to embark on a journey. No matter how resilient you are and how many milestones you have achieved, some amount of anxiety will always attack you.

Like change, fears and anxiety are inevitable and never really leave your side. Now that you know that, you should also know that you could learn how to manage them better and equip yourself with the confidence, courage, and strength you need to control your fear and anxiety and prevent them from exacerbating.

Once you have a better grip on your anxiety, apprehensions, and fears, you can move past your comfort zone and courageously take risks in life as well as explore new things.

In this section, we will talk about both aspects in detail.

The Importance of Managing Your Anxiety and Fears (and How to)

Over the years, fear and anxiety have received a bad rap. While your worries/fears certainly have the power to cripple you mentally and obstruct your progress, a certain amount of fear helps you stay safe too. You need to differentiate between the two and build the ability to spot the two types of fears at the right time.

Here is how you can attain this ability and ensure your unnecessary fears stop getting in the way of accomplishing your goals.

1. Every time you feel paralyzed by fear, acknowledge the occurrence. Talk about your situation and the fear in detail. Discuss how it makes you anxious and how it is obstructing your progress. Dig into its details and analyze how it influences your goals and achievements.

2. Next, go over the fears a few times and try to be as unbiased as possible. This helps you understand whether you are rationally analyzing the situation or just catastrophizing for no good reason. Catastrophizing a situation refers to thinking of the worst-case scenario and blowing a situation out of proportion without any solid

justification. For instance, if you are nervous about your businesses' launch event, you may worry to the extent that you fear no participant will show up, and the event will be a disaster. The problem with this approach is that it pulls you deep into negative thinking to the extent that you think of nothing else. When you do this, you draw negative experiences your way and eventually shape your fears into reality. Therefore, it is best not to catastrophize an event.

3. If you find yourself becoming extremely worried about an issue, list down your worries and question their authenticity. If you fear you will fail an exam, what are the odds of that happening? If the odds are high, why is it that? Is it because you have not studied at all? If that is the case, start studying now to equalize the odds. When you analyze the real problem at hand, you become capable of dealing with it objectively, and you eliminate the overwhelming element from the situation, which makes it easier to deal with the problem.

4. Try to become solution-focused instead of problem-focused. Whatever your fears are, accept them, and pay attention to them so that you can identify how to solve the issue. Anxiety comes from lacking a real-time and effective solution. When you reflect on exactly how to mitigate a problem, the apprehensiveness associated with it vanishes too.

5. If a certain fear seems rational and is likely to protect you from trouble, accept it and try not to do that thing. For instance, if you realize you are not prepared to take part in a certain trade exhibition because you have not prepared enough for it, drop the idea. Participating in it may end up in a disaster and create more mess for you; it is, therefore, better to avoid the havoc beforehand.

6. Work on constantly increasing your self-confidence by feeding on uplifting suggestions. Tell yourself day in and day out how amazing, confident, and successful you are, and how you have the power and ability to take on any challenge and face your fears. When your subconscious hears these suggestions repeatedly, it eventually embraces them and turns you into a fearless person.

7. As you work on training your mind to squash fear, you need to work on building your skillset too. Figure out the skills or potential you lack that keeps you from taking on certain challenges and then hone on it. If you cannot sell your marketing program in trade fairs because you fear public speaking, build this skill now. When you know you can overcome a certain challenge, the fear associated with it dissipates away too.

As you gain the ability to control your anxiety and fears, enduring challenges will become a piece of cake for you. You then need to work on moving past your comfort zone so you can explore your potential and constantly expand it to become a better version of yourself with time.

The Comfort Zone: Find Yours, Bust the Wall and Expand It

We have that one space or place in our lives where we feel extremely comfortable and can relax peacefully. It could be your home, your garden, or any other place where you go to feel like yourself.

Similarly, we all have a mental space where we feel so comfortable that often, we do not want to leave it or move past it. This is the comfort zone related to our capabilities, goals, potentials, and challenges. Mental zones are the mental boundaries we set for ourselves beyond which we do not really feel like going.

There is no point in being mentally tough if you will always reside within your comfort zone. You cannot grow your potential if you keep lurking within the same area repeatedly. Mental toughness allows you to bust the walls of your comfort zone and become a tougher version of yourself.

Here is how you can do it:

1. First, delve into the reasons behind your comfort zone. What made you build those walls in the first place? Once you know what led to the creation of the comfort zone, you can work on those areas and keep it from growing. A comfort zone is normally a result of fears such as the fears of failing, struggling, and not growing. Since you are by now better aware of your fears, you can tackle them so that you can move a step closer to busting your comfort zone.

2. Second, you need to understand how staying in that comfort zone is limiting your growth. If you aspire to be the best legal advisor in the country, but you only take on cases with the least amount of risks involved, you will never learn how to battle difficult scenarios, which will always cause obstruction to your goal.

3. Third, think of what lies beyond your comfort zone and how breaking free from the comfort zone will really add value to your life. For instance, think of how taking on high-risk cases will hone on your potential and turn you into the finest legal advisor the country has ever seen. This will prove your mettle to the world and make everyone bow down to your glory. When you think of it this way, your motivation grows, and you feel strong enough to move outside your comfort zone.

4. Next, list down the baby steps you can take to move closer to your goals and start working on them right now one-step at a time. This slow and steady approach to expanding your comfort zone is the best way to go about this goal.

5. On every step, enjoy the phase and the process that takes you to the final goal, audit your progress, and improve yourself so that you move further towards your final destination.

If you practice this, in a few weeks' time, you will find yourself becoming stronger and more competent than ever. This will help you build and grow your willpower and self-discipline muscles.

The next section talks about how to grow your self-discipline and willpower muscles even further:

Section 7

Self-Discipline and Willpower- How to Build and Grow It

"the willingness to show up changes us. it makes us a little braver each time."

—

BRENÉ BROWN

Self-discipline is the muscle all of us need to build to ensure we do what is right and important and that we never give in to our temptations. When you are working on a new goal, you need to prepare yourself to fulfill that commitment not just once or twice, but every single day.

The reason why many of us fail to fulfill our New Year's Resolutions is not that we lack the potential to fulfill them or because the resolutions do not hold meaning for us. The reason is that we lack the self-discipline we need to have to strive for our goals regularly and *not just once or twice.* When we realize the amount of effort and discipline that goes into the success process, we often panic and decide to quit the goal altogether. This will not happen if we have the discipline to fuel your willpower constantly until you actualize your goals.

Your willpower is the ability to keep your mind calm and thinking rationally during challenging times; being disciplined means being able to take consistent actions that help you achieve your target and battle all your temptations. When you have great willpower, you can build and grow your level of self-discipline.

This section shall outline all the strategies you can use to build and grow your willpower and self-discipline. Let's see what you need to do to accomplish this target.

Iron Tough Willpower: How to Acquire It

Think of every time you must train in the gym but feel tempted to snuggle up in your cozy bed. If you give in to your temptation of going back to bed instead of training, it is clear you have a weak willpower.

Your willpower refers to your ability to stay composed every time adversity or challenge comes your way. If your willpower is weak, your negative and distracting thoughts will take over your ability to think rationally. Every time you have a distracting thought, you will pay heed to it and react to it. This explains why you fall short of becoming mentally tough and why you fail at being the champion of your life.

If you implement the following strategies, you will eventually build the willpower you need to stay strong.

1. Begin with becoming more aware of your thoughts.

2. If you are thinking of doing a certain task, pay attention to all the thoughts orbiting your mind and look for any thoughts that debilitate your confidence, relate to your fears, or remind you of your temptations.

3. Acknowledge those thoughts and jot them down on paper.

4. Think of the repercussions you would face if you succumb to your distractions. If you do not work on preparing your business plan now, think of how you will be unable to apply for grants later, how you will financial institutions will deny you funding, and how you may not be able to structure and organize your business properly because of it.

5. Think of how things would improve for you if you do what you need to do. If you are struggling between your desire to hang out with friends and your professional obligation to write your business plan, think of how you had dedicated this time to working on the business plan and how it would prove to be bountiful for your business in the future.

6. Take deep breaths and use positive suggestions to replace your negative, tempting thoughts. Chant the positive suggestions repeatedly until you start feeling strong from within.

Implement these guidelines every time you feel the urge to engage in a tempting task that distracts you from your mission. If you work on these tips consistently, you will notice yourself becoming mentally stronger and tougher.

In addition to the above, you also need to understand that your willpower depletes when you fail to engage in two practices that help sustain and grow your willpower.

First, you need to rest your mind after engaging in a difficult task. If you have convinced yourself to work on your business plan, and have now started creating it, after three hours of work, relax for an hour at least. If you push your mind to constantly engage in tough work for hours and hours, you will feel exhausted and unconsciously experience the urge to give in to your temptations. Make sure that does not happen by taking time-outs after working on difficult tasks.

Second, you need to accompany your willpower with empowering actions that help you stay strong amidst challenges. If you only tell yourself of how working out is beneficial for you but do not get up and hit the treadmill, if you just keep sitting on the bed, you will eventually lie down and fall asleep. You need to get up and take meaningful actions that prove your positive thoughts right. This is where building your self-discipline muscle comes in handy.

Self-Discipline: What It Means, What it Takes and How to Get It

Tai Lopez is an investor, advisor, consultant, and a self-help, motivational speaker. He has created the 67 Steps program through which he aims to help people build and live a good life characterized by love, health, wealth, and happiness. In his program, he repeatedly mentions how to achieve your targets you need to take powerful, result-yielding action consistently and not just once.

The writers who have bestsellers to their credit do not write a few thousand words one day and do nothing for days to come. They sit down at a certain hour of the day *every day*; they think about their project and write stuff down. The athletes who have bagged gold medals at international championships do not just engage in high-intensity and strength training exercises a few days of the month; they do it every single day. Businesspersons who have built multimillion-dollar enterprises did not just do it courtesy of a stroke of luck. They worked hard for their goals every single day. This is how accomplishments happen. and this is what you need to do, as well.

Willpower alone is not enough to pull you through obstacles or help you rise above the challenge. You need self-discipline as well, and if you incorporate the following strategies in your life, you too, can achieve this target.

1. Think of your goal and reflect on all the bad habits that keep you from achieving it. If your goal is to write one book of 30,000 words in two months, think of the bad habits preventing you from achieving that target. It could be your habit of procrastination, of working for a few hours a day only, of thinking negatively, or anything else.

2. Acknowledge the bad habit and identify the habit loop that causes you to stick to those practices. A habit loop comprises of the habit reminder, habit routine, and habit reward; this loop is what causes you to engage in that exercise repeatedly. A reminder is anything that triggers that habit; it could be time, action, thought, person, etc. The routine is the way you carry out a certain practice, and the reward refers to the emotional or physical reward you receive from engaging in that exercise. If you smoke after every meal as a way to relax and digest the meal, eating a meal is the trigger that causes the bad habit; smoking two

cigarettes in the garage is the routine, and feeling relaxed is the reward you enjoy from smoking.

3. Observe the bad habit that serves as the hurdle in your road to success and look for the habit reminder, routine, and reward. You then need to work on avoiding the triggers for a while and doing more positive, healthier habits every time you encounter a certain reminder. If your goal is to become healthier and physically fit, but you are in the habit of lying down after every meal, get up and take a light stroll 10 minutes after having a meal.

4. Think about the habits that would provide you with the same reward offered by the bad habit; this will help ensure you do not feel as if you are missing out. If you smoke to relax, maybe talk to a helpful friend, take a warm bath, or read something soothing that helps you beat away stress.

5. As you work on breaking your bad habits, you will build the inner resistance and self-control you need to work on your milestones with discipline. When this happens, make sure you work on your action plan and take meaningful action daily.

6. Moreover, every time you exercise your willpower to avoid a temptation, make sure you do something that helps you fulfill your goal. If you talked yourself into doing 20 reps instead of 10, go the extra mile and do those 10 additional reps.

7. Enlist the different tasks that help boost your productivity and achieve a certain target. Of that lot, pick the toughest task and decide to work on it so that you can build your self-discipline. We call this *"eating an ugly frog,"* a brilliant hack that you can use skyrocket your productivity. If putting up your business's stall in a crafts fair will give it the visibility it needs to improve sales, but

you fear it may not go well, set up a stall anyway. When you eat an ugly frog, you feel self-assured and know you can meet any challenge. This helps grow your willpower and level of discipline.

It takes courage and resilience to overcome temptations, but once you do that, you turn into the finest, most amazing version of yourself. This also gives you the strength to handle failures, bounce back to action after stumbling a few times, and build a champion's mindset.

The next section of the book elaborates this further.

Section 8

*Building a Champion's Mindset and
Handling Failures*

> I think anything is
> possible if you have the
> mindset and the will and
> desire to do it and put
> the time in.
>
> – Roger Clemens.

"Champions are not born; they are built over time." They persevere in difficult times, putting a constant leash on their temptations, they are strong and resilient, and do not give adversities a chance to get the better of them. All the

tactics, tips, and hacks we have studied in the previous sections help you instill those abilities.

In this section, we are going to recap all that you have learned so far so that you can gain better clarity on how to handle failures, how to build a champion's mindset, and how to develop habits of successful people.

How to Handle Failure: Bounce Back, Forge Through and Embrace Failures

If you do not bounce back every time a challenge comes roaring your way, you will give your fears a chance to cripple you for good. That is not how we make a champion, is it now?

Since you are aware that you have it in you to make it big, you owe it to your talents and dreams, and to yourself to make your mark on the world. To handle failure well, in addition to implementing the guidelines taught in the previous sections, observe the following tips too.

1. **Befriend the Failures:** Earlier, we looked at how to change your perception of setbacks. Well, every time adversity knocks on your door, you need to do exactly that. Instead of viewing setbacks as your enemies, perceive them as your friends. What does a friend do when times are tough? He/she guides and supports you, right? Sometimes, your friend's advice may seem harsh, but he/she only has your best interests at heart. Understand that the failures you encounter in life want the same for you. They may present you with difficulties, but the aim of those difficulties is to help you grow and flourish. The instant you adopt this outlook towards failures, you stop finding them scary at all.

2. Do not Judge and Label Failures as Bad Episodes: A major reason why setbacks in life upset you is that you attach judgments and labels to them. If you view a setback as a testament of your incompetence and see it as an unfortunate event, you will empower it, and it will scare you. Every time you encounter a failure, do not view it as something bad. Instead, view it as a routine occurrence that happened due to some of your shortcomings and due to uncontrollable factors beyond your reach. When you stop judging a failure, your approach towards it softens too.

3. Learn from Failure: A failure has a lot more teach you than a victory. When you stop judging the setbacks you experience, you adopt a positive attitude towards them. This helps you identify the shortcomings that led to the unfortunate outcome, which helps you improve on them. Learning from your failures and experiences helps you overcome your weaknesses and hone your potentials so that, with time, you become a better version of yourself.

4. Have a Positive Support System: Every successful person in the world has the support and backing of loved ones who helped his or her bounce back during difficult times. Warren Buffet had the support of his wife and friend; Mark Zuckerberg is always thankful to his wife for supporting him through everything, and Stephen King owes the success of his first novel to his wife, who encouraged him to pursue his passion after scores of publishers rejected his book proposals. Similarly, to fight back your challenges and become successful, you need the love and encouragement of some positive influences in your life. Figure out the genuinely caring people in your social circle and spend more time with them. Replace them with all those who put you down, criticize you incessantly, and make fun of your ideas. Once there are fewer naysayers in your life, and you spend a large portion of your time surrounded by positive influences, you will feel more inspired to progress in life.

Once you start handling your failures with courage and grace, you slowly inculcate the champion's mindset. Here are a few more things you need to do to build and sustain a champion's mindset.

A Champion's Mindset: How the World's Winners Think and Habits of Successful People

The world's winners think differently, which is why we often refer to them as "accomplished people." It takes a lot more than courage and optimism to get where you want to be.

Let us look at what goes into shaping a champion's mindset and what successful people across the globe do to ensure they actualize their goals and become mentally tough.

1. **They have specific goals:** When a champion sets a goal, he/she is very specific about what he/she wants. Instead of saying, "I want more money," he/she specifies how much. Instead of just wanting physical fitness, a champion describes his/her idea of physical fitness. When you are specific about what you want, you train your mind to think about that goal and shape your actions accordingly. Take Arnold Schwarzenegger's example. When he wanted to be a bodybuilder, he knew exactly why he wanted a muscular body because he wanted to win championships and go to America. Being specific is what helped him work hard because his goal was as clear as day.

2. They think in terms of minutes: When accomplished people schedule and assign tasks, they think in terms of minutes; this helps them make sure they minimize time wastage and optimize their productivity. Elon Musk has a regimented schedule that sees him chunk his entire calendar into several 5-minute slots. Mark Zuckerberg decided to stick to wearing a grey T-shirt daily to save time spent on worrying about what to wear. When you must plan your work, think in terms of minutes so that you do not spend a minute more doing something meaningless.

3. They focus on continuous learning: Observe any champion you know, and you will quickly realize that this person has a habit of continuously learning new things. Champions have a hunger to grow and learn; because of it, they read more, take lessons and workshops, watch worthwhile videos, and constantly aim to broaden their skillset. According to Bill Gates, one of the chief ways through which he has learned a lot in life is to read more books. Accomplished people never think they know enough; instead, they focus on learning as much as possible. If you wish to climb up the success ladder constantly, you, too, need to inculcate this habit.

4. They enhance their emotional intelligence: Successful people value emotional intelligence and are aware of the significance of being emotionally strong. One of their key habits is to shape up their emotional intelligence consistently by learning to balance work and play, eliminating distractions, embracing change, being empathetic, going with the flow, not chasing perfectionism, becoming self-motivated, focusing on finding the good points in the worst-case scenarios, and by setting boundaries. Take Oprah Winfrey's example, for instance.

She credits her success to her ability to handle her emotions and constantly grow her emotional strength.

5. **They think realistically positive:** According to Sophia Chou, a successful organizational psychology researcher working at the National Taiwan University, accomplished people in the world think realistically positive. Every time they encounter a setback, they do not think they are out of options. Instead, they realistically analyze the situation and approach the setback optimistically; this helps them find a solution.

6. **They meditate regularly:** What do Jennifer Aniston, a renowned Hollywood actress, Oprah Winfrey, a successful TV show host, Adam Levine, lead singer of Maroon V (musical band), and Tony Robbins, self-help guru, and motivational speaker extraordinaire have in common? All of them advocate for meditating regularly and making a habit out of doing so as well. Meditation soothes your racing mind, improves your level of focus, helps you understand your genuine aspirations, and increases your level of mindfulness. This strengthens your resilience, emotional strength, mental toughness, and grit.

7. **They stumble but never budge from their stance:** Every champion you revere and look up to always knew that he/she will not succeed at every goal and that some failures are inevitable. Despite this fact, he/she kept moving forward, and even when he/she stumbled, he/she got back up. This is how all champions eventually objectify their goals. Successful people do not perceive their setbacks as the end of the road. They learn from failures and use those experiences to improve and grow. They are in the habit of staying committed to their goals, and despite stumbling several times, they never give up.

8. **They create time to achieve their goals by improving their time management skills:** People often wonder how successful people do so much in the same 24 hours everyone has. It is not because they possess a secret magic wand; it is because of their excellent time management skills. When a winner takes on another goal, he/she does not think how his/her plate is already full. If he/she believes in the goal, he/she is ready to take on the challenge and creates time for it. By creating priorities, discerning between high and low priority tasks, identifying peak energy time, eliminating distractions, scheduling tasks, and breaking up difficult tasks into smaller, doable targets, the champions can achieve their goals. This is how they seamlessly move from one milestone to another, whereas the complainers only continue to whine and crib about how they never have enough time to do anything. If you want to be the winner that you deserve to be, start making time for the goals you value.

9. **They take accountability for their actions and create their success:** Successful people do not expect the world to benefit them or provide them with success. Steve Jobs experienced many obstacles in his life and even had to leave college because of financial constraints. Despite all the adversities, he never blamed the situation or expected anyone to help him out. He kept working hard to pursue his passion for IT and, eventually, he created Apple Inc. Accomplished people strongly believe that they can achieve their targets through their work ethic, commitment, and beliefs, and they make sure to do that by taking full responsibility for their actions.

10. **They know when to pull the plug:** When many people often give in to the temptation to stick to something that is not working for a few more weeks, the

accomplished people have this innate ability to understand the right time to pursue a goal and the right time to quit it. This is because of their healthy habit of digging deeper into the matter and being aware of different aspects related to a situation. If they invest in a business, they stay aware of the industry trends, corporate sector, and any legislation passed. Due to their ability to stay aware and eagerness to learn, they quickly realize when a certain pursuit is a complete wastage of resources and time.

11. **They nurture gratitude:** Jim Carrey, the successful comedian we adore and look up to now, had a very difficult life. Like many others, he had humble beginnings and had to do several odd jobs before landing a role in a Hollywood movie. While life may not have been easy on him, Carrey never stopped being grateful for what he had. He advises everyone to nurture gratitude because that is what helped him stay optimistic in difficult times and power through every obstacle. Gratitude is another virtue commonly found in all successful people. Successful people are aware of their blessings and constantly express their gratitude for these blessings.

12. **They are passionate about their work:** Accomplished people have a habit of infusing passion in their work. Most of them have turned their passions into their work because when passion becomes work, nothing seems difficult or impossible. However, since you cannot always earn a living from your passion, you can always inject enthusiasm into the work that helps you earn your bread and butter. Successful people acknowledge that and pay heed to this. To be successful, you need to realize your passions and then develop the necessary skills to pursue them and turn them into thriving professions.

13. **They journal a lot:** J. K. Rowling, Jack Dorsey, Eminem, Drew Hansen, and Richard Branson all always carry notebooks with them and use these notebooks to jot down their thoughts and ideas regularly. This helps them set goals, track their progress, and easily reflect on their feelings and lessons so that they can improve in life. Dorsey rightfully once said, *"Find a simple way to track your progress. You really get to see how you have grown, how your business has grown, and how your own leadership has grown."* You know you are amazing and cut out for some amazing goals in this life. You only need to believe in your power and set compelling goals accordingly. Always keep a journal with you, and take it out to pen down your thoughts, feelings, and emotions towards all areas of your life. Record your performance in it regularly and go through the accounts at the end of the day. Join the dots between different instances so that you can explore and understand yourself better and make the most of that learning.

14. **They take risks:** If playing safe was the way to achieve big goals, you would not see any successful people. Accomplishments do not come easily. They come with hard work, perseverance, and taking risks. Richard Branson once put every tiny bit of the property he owned, including his house on risk to fund a certain project. All his partners bailed out of it because of the high stakes involved, but Branson believed in the cause, and his risk turned out to be his biggest success to date. Virgin Records incurred massive growth after that and to this day, Branson recalls that experience with pride and gratitude. You need to become a risk-taker as well, because high rewards only come with high risks. Remember that sometimes, "you cannot cross a chasm in two small jumps."

As you can see, successful people think and behave in a certain way. This way, and their positive habits, is what invites success their way. You, too, need to adopt the same attitude towards your goals so that you can become the winner you have always envisaged yourself as.

Conclusion

Nobody has it "all figured out." None of the successful people in the world always knew where they would land or how to achieve a certain goal. All most of them had is a yearning desire to prove their worth, and they kept looking for answers around them. They explored themselves and determined what they wanted and what brought them meaning. Therefore, they never settled for anything less than they believed they deserved and worked hard to strive for their goals.

To continuously improve yourself and become an incredibly mentally tough version of yourself, you need to adopt the same mentality in life. Fortunately, you have all the guidelines packed in this book to help you accomplish your goals.

Believe in yourself and vehemently implement the various growth hacks we have discussed because they will help you accomplish all your goals!

References

https://www.wikihow.com/Become-Stronger-Emotionally

https://www.inc.com/kevin-daum/9-ways-to-build-your-inner-strength.html

https://www.forbes.com/sites/chrismyers/2017/10/06/the-40-rule-the-simple-secret-to-success/#702b4eb35cdd

https://trainingindustry.com/articles/strategy-alignment-and-planning/3-steps-to-development-that-helps-you-move-past-your-limiting-beliefs/

https://tinybuddha.com/blog/3-things-that-limit-your-potential-and-how-to-overcome-them/

https://thehustle.co/40-percent-rule-navy-seal-secret-mental-toughness

https://www.inc.com/business-insider/13-secrets-to-performing-well-under-pressure.html

http://mentalfloss.com/article/72706/11-secrets-performing-well-under-pressure

https://www.forbes.com/sites/forbescoachescouncil/2017/07/28/18-ways-to-get-better-at-working-under-pressure/#6ab94ab62e35 https://www.inc.com/lolly-daskal/how-to-make-yourself-mentally-strong-this-year.html https://www.inc.com/lolly-daskal/how-to-make-yourself-mentally-strong-this-year.html

https://www.intellectualtakeout.org/article/mentally-weak-people-often-have-these-3-habits

https://www.huffpost.com/entry/10-useful-ways-to-choose-the-right-direction-in-life_b_9192982

https://www.awesomeinventions.com/mentally-strong-people/

https://spacepipen.wordpress.com/2015/01/18/weak-minded-vs-strong-minded-people/#targetText=Then%20who%20are%20weak%2Dminded,up%20fast%20and%20are%20pessimistic.

https://www.google.com/search?sxsrf=ACYBGNTH5tPkgCrZjfgOMJ7IY4aebDf2ZA%3A1571518079351&source=hp&ei=f3arXe2FE7GMlwSUmpmgDw&q=strong+mindset+versus+weak+mindset&oq=strong+mindset+versus+weak+mindset&gs_l=psy-ab.3...27.6121..6543...0.0..0.394.8905.2-31j3......0....1..gws-wiz.......0j0i131j35i39j0i10j0i70i255j0i22i30j0i22i10i30j33i21j33i22i29i30j33i160j33i10.96yqXMHhJ9I&ved=0ahUKEwitwYCHmanlAhUxxoUKHRRNBvQQ4dUDCAY&uact=5

https://www.ancient-origins.net/history-ancient-traditions/spartan-soldiers-0011616

https://life.spartan.com/post/9-ways-to-live-like-a-spartan-soldier

http://ignorelimits.com/spartan-habits/

https://jamesclear.com/mental-toughness

https://www.inc.com/peter-economy/12-thoughts-of-todays-most-highly-successful-people.html

---

https://www.entrepreneur.com/article/293944

https://www.businessinsider.com/how-successful-people-think-john-maxwell-2011-9#figure-out-where-you-need-to-focus-your-energy-and-then-use-the-8020-rule-2

Part 2: Stoicism

Unlock the Secrets to a Stoic Life, Emotional Resilience and an Unshakeable Mindset and Discover Principles, Mindfulness Meditation Techniques and Habits for Bulletproof Calmness in Chaos

Introduction

What is stoicism?

Stoicism is a philosophy of life that was designed to enable individuals to live their lives the best way possible. This philosophy helps to lower negative emotions, maximizes positive feelings, and enables people to focus and work on their virtues of character. Stoicism is applicable at all stages of life and all moments. There is a framework provided for living each moment and each stage of life. People get reminded of things that are actually important in life, and they get to learn about practical strategies that will enable them to get what is really valuable in life.

Greco-Roman Philosophy

History of stoicism

Stoicism is a philosophy that was founded in 301 BC by Zeno, a philosopher from the city of Citium which is modern-day Cyprus. The philosophy obtains its name from a public market where stoics met in Athens. This public market was known as 'Stoa Poikile' which means "painted porch".

Stoics met here and held lengthy but interesting discussions with all other interested participants. The discussions that included stoics and all other interested people were philosophical. It is through these discussions that doctrines of stoicism were developed.

Another prominent figure in the development and advancement of stoicism is Chrysippus. This gentleman is credited with eloquently developing the doctrines of stoicism and is part of the "early Stoa".

The Stoics were influenced greatly by early philosophers and thinkers. They were especially influenced by the Cynics and by Socrates as well as skeptics and academics. The academics were mostly followers of the great thinker and philosopher, Plato.

Beyond this initial stage in the development of stoicism is the second stage which is known as the "middle Stoa". One of the more popular philosophers at the initial and second stages is Cicero. He was not necessarily a Stoic but simply a sympathetic thinker. He was one of the major developers of the thinking that developed the doctrines of Stoa. It was also during this stage that stoicism was introduced to Rome.

The "late Stoa" period is the last stage in the development of this philosophy. This stage happened during the imperial reign of the Roman Empire. However, stoicism experienced a decline when Christianity became the main religion across the Roman Empire. Other schools of thought also went into decline such as Epicureanism.

As Christianity spread across the Roman Empire and stoicism began to fade, some famous historical figures stuck with the idea because it influenced them greatly even though some were critics of the philosophy. Those who were influenced by it include Thomas Aquinas, Thomas

Moore, Francis Bacon, Erasmus Boethius, and other Fathers of the early church.

Other entities were also influenced by this way of life including neo-orthodox protestant theology and modern existentialism. Stoicism is seeing a resurgence and influencing plenty of practices including cognitive behavior and logotherapy. There are rather many similarities between stoicism and other philosophical approaches such as secular humanism and Buddhism.

Stoicism's three areas of study

According to the Stoics, the most crucial aspect of their philosophy was practical ethics. Practical ethics speaks about living the best life that a person could live. Even then, they determined that other additional components were necessary to affect the ethics aspect. These additional aspects are the understanding of how the world functions as well as acceptance of the limitations as well as the capacity of human thinking.

As such, stoicism principles are based on three main aspects: logic, physics, and ethics. In stoicism, physics here refers to natural philosophy, metaphysics, and natural science. Ancient philosophers were very aware of the limitation of human wisdom and knowledge and hence were always ready and willing to change their views. This is why, over time, some aspects of stoicism were overtaken by modern knowledge, including science.

When it comes to logic, stoics often include aspects epistemology which is a theory of knowledge as well as psychology and other relevant social sciences. They came up with a logic belief system that strongly opposed that which had earlier been put forward by Aristotle.

Philosophy and ethics

Most people are interested in learning about stoic ethics rather than the logic and physics aspects of it. This is because stoic ethics is closely related to practical philosophy. Many people are of the opinion that stoicism is about disguising emotions and living life with concealed feelings.

The truth is that stoics learn how to turn their emotions around so they can attain inner peace. Certain situations that humans experience every day cause different types of emotions, including love, anger, and fear. Fortunately, we can learn how to avoid negative emotions by using the reflective mind. Using the reflective mind, we can set aside the emotions and then take the time to consider whether the emotions should be appreciated or discarded.

Stoics can clearly distinguish between acting based on sound judgment and instinctive reactions. The former is referred to as "eupathos" while the latter is known as "propathos". The aim of stoics is to attain peace of mind based on sound judgment after assessing a situation or incident. This peace of mind status is referred to as "apatheia".

The stoics believed that a successful and flourishing life is one where a person develops moral virtues in order to become a decent human and good member of society. In this regard, they developed four distinct cardinal virtues: courage, wisdom, temperance, and justice.

Positive action for any situation

Stoicism provides a solution for living an excellent life regardless of a given situation or the stage in life that one is at. People are made to think and consider what things are honorable, decent, and truly important so they can apply what is decent and honorable.

Stoicism is designed deliberately to add value to life, be actionable, and make sense. In fact, no one needs to learn any new meditation techniques or philosophical theories. Stoicism simply offers practical, beneficial, and instant ways of improving a person's character and finding peace and tranquility in simple yet practical ways.

Reasons for the development of stoicism

Back in the third century BC, a school of philosophy developed. It originated from Ancient Rome and Greece at a time when people were really focused on leading meaningful lives devoid of drudgery and misery. Back then, people never thought that attaining material things such as money or personal glory and prestige would result in happiness. Most were focused on ways through which they could attain peace and happiness.

This is where stoicism derived its school of thought. Stoicism provided solutions to challenges like fear, stress, anxiety, and major questions people have—such as what they want out of life. The main answer to most of these challenges was, "I desire peace of mind and continuous happiness all which come from being a person of virtue."

All these were attained through a practical approach. An individual seeking to improve the virtues of character needed to focus more on their actions rather than words. Basically, positive actions lead to positive experiences and a better quality of life and a challenging experience results from negative behavior.

In brief, we can conclude that stoicism is an ancient philosophy and school of thought that focuses on a specific way of living. Its main focus is on how to reduce negative emotions, maximize happiness, and generally lead a virtuous life. Plenty of renowned individuals across the world have tested these principles including Tom Brady, Thomas Jefferson, and George Washington.

Four cardinal values

Stoics believe in the four distinct virtues of justice, courage, temperance, and wisdom. This is because a good life, according to the stoics, was found through the development of one's moral virtues. Stoics believe that cultivating proper moral values lead a person to become good and morally upright.

Also, stoics took great care regarding certain aspects, including health and wealth. These and other goods should not be allowed to affect a person's morality. In essence, a person can be morally upright regardless of the status of their wealth, health, or status in society. Even then, some of these things aid in achieving stoic objectives so they are preferable while others may not be preferred as they are a hindrance.

Stoic followers make a big distinction between matters within their control and matters outside their control. One of these issues is the thought process. Our attitudes and thoughts feature here in a major way. The basic plan here is that peace of mind is as a result of focusing on matters that are within our control and setting aside things not within our control. Things outside of our control should not cause us to worry or expend emotions on; there is no need to despair or get concerned about things that you have no control over.

A majority of early stoics were prominent members of the community. They included emperors, military generals, and politicians. This means that they expended their energies each day attempting to change society in order to make it better for us all. Even then, they accepted that there are things that they could not change and so made peace with that fact.

Stoics accepted that their philosophy is one of love, and as such, they learned and accepted how to love and accept not just themselves but others as well. Love should also not be limited to only close friends and family. Stoics have a general love towards humankind and nature as well. The view of stoics was to improve the state of humanity and the world.

How to apply stoic principles

So how do stoics practice stoicism? There are certain practices and procedures. The most prominent of these are certain spiritual exercises that are greatly inspired by ancient writings. Different people approach stoicism differently, but the basic principles are the same across the board. Here are some common stoic practices:

1. *Morning meditation.* The first activity of the day should be meditation. You should find a nice and quiet place where you can spend some moments meditating. The spot you choose should not be too brightly lit. It does not have to be outdoors but a spot even in your home that is comfortable and quiet.

As you meditate, take time to focus on your day ahead and think about the virtues and doctrines of stoicism. Sometimes stoics also focus on certain sayings from the ancient philosophers like Socrates. Read one or two and think about it, then try and live according to the saying.

2. *Make use of Hierocles' Circle.* The Hierocle's Circle allows for visual exercises which are also great for stoics. The circle requires you to think about certain things in a certain order. You first think about yourself and then

extend the thoughts to your family, friends, and close circle. You also think about the residents of your city, your neighbors and people where you work and live. You finally extend this circle and think about the people of this world, nature, and eventually the entire universe.

3. *View from above:* Also take a view of yourself like before, but this time, from an aerial view. Expand this circle and think about your country, the sky, clusters of galaxies, and the entire universe.

Chapter 1: Everything You Need to be Happy is Found Within

According to the principles of stoicism, everything that you need to be truly happy lies within you. As it is, you only need to focus on the things which you can change without worrying about those which you cannot change.

Remember that stoicism is all about living your best life possible. This can begin at any point in a person's life. According to stoicism, you need very little in order to be happy. This is because everything that you need to be happy can be found within. According to stoics, the secret to happiness is really simple.

Ideally, and as already mentioned, we do not control the things that happen to us. As such, we should not expend energy, thought, or time on matters beyond our control. This is what stoicism is all about. By not focusing on things beyond our control, we avoid unnecessary tension, stress, worry, and anxiety.

Stoicism

Of all the philosophies of ancient times, stoicism is among those that focus on the happiness and wellbeing of the individual. People across the world have lately been taking a keen interest in the works of three stoic philosophers: Marcus Aurelius, who was an emperor, Epictetus, who was initially a slave, and Seneca, a popular tutor to Nero.

Stoics basically share one underlying principle—they believe that stoicism is the solution to a happy and stress-free life and this is achieved through the attainment of an excellent state of mind. This kind of mental state is obtained by being rational and with virtue. A great life is one where an individual is at peace with nature.

Stoicism started in Greece and was founded by a philosopher known as Zeno in 300 BC. Stoicism obtained its name from the 'Painted Stoa', which is a location in Athens where Zeno used to teach. Sadly, most of the works of early stoics were lost, so people now focus on the teachings of Roman stoics.

Happiness and unhappiness

Epictetus expressed a couple of ideas that have provided foundation principles on stoicism and happiness. According to Epictetus, there are things that we can control and things beyond our control. According to him, there is very little in life that we can control. For instance, we do not have control over what people do or say to us, we are not able to really control what happens to us, and we also do not completely control our bodies—which do become sick and eventually die without any due consideration to our thoughts and feelings.

The few things that we do have control over include the judgments and opinions we make regarding things and the way we think about different issues. He then goes on to state that situations and things do not upset people and make them sad, but it is more about what we think about these things. For instance, let us assume something significant occurs. As human beings, we can come up with our own thoughts about the things that just occurred.

Situations, incidents, and occurrences are in and of themselves neutral by nature. This is because that which might upset you is quite harmless to others. Others even welcome some situations. According to stoicism principles, it is the individual conclusions that we arrive at after a situation or incident that may cause us to be either happy or unhappy.

Stoicism dictates that we have control over the thought process regarding these occurrences and the conclusions we arrive at. Due to this, our happiness is strictly based on the conclusions we make about the things that happen to us. As it is, things do happen. When they do, they could be good or bad depending on how we view them or rather how we choose to value them.

From a distance, it may sound like underestimating the serious challenges that individuals encounter daily. For example, how can altering the way we think help put food on someone's table? Even then, the early stoics were not afraid of tackling such questions and actually acknowledged that and admitted that life could indeed be difficult and challenging.

Take the example of Seneca, one of the early stoics. He went through plenty of suffering, including multiple bereavements as well as being exiled. He was eventually forced to take his own life by Emperor Nero.

Practical exercises

With time, the stoics developed a number of exercises whose main purpose was to assist in training individuals on how to adapt stoic ideas into their everyday lives. One of the recommendations came from Seneca himself. According to him, it is a great idea to take stock of each day and note instances when you become angry or lash out at someone who possibly does not deserve it. If you can note such mistakes, then you will observe what triggered it and possibly react differently next time.

Another strategy that was adopted by the stoics was developed by Marcus Aurelius. He was always alert to the fact that he would likely encounter plenty of angry people throughout the day. Most of these would be angry, ungrateful, impatient and probably stressed out individuals. It is advisable to consider the feelings of others and understand that most people are stressed and possibly unhappy. As such, it is advisable to be prepared for negative contact with people and hence avoid conflict.

Stoics also teach that we are rather unimportant. As things are, human beings are quite dispensable, and the universe does not revolve around us. During meditation, most stoics focused on the vastness of the universe as well as the infinity of time. Time does stretch way into the past and deep into the future. In comparison to this vastness, our lives are minute and simple moments. As such, if you expect the universe to hand you what you want, then you will be disappointed. However, if you learn to accept whatever the universe dishes out, then you will be much more content with life.

Develop a morning ritual

Stoics have learned to embrace a concept known as 'Amor Fati'. This concept teaches us to accept all that life hands us, whether bad or good, and to embrace it, revel in it, and love it. This means embracing even moments that are tough, challenging, awful, and regrettable.

There are many moments in life when things are tough, when numerous challenges arise, and things simply suck. At such times, we tend to feel really down and dejected, which is not a very good thing. However, we should not let any negative feelings and challenges in life pull us down. It is advisable to understand that life will always have its challenges and difficulties. As such, it is advisable to accept the things that happen to us. Acceptance, they say, is the best solution of handling and dealing with the tough situations that life hands us.

Plenty of people walk around hoping that life will give them everything that they need on a silver platter. Many of us hope and pray that life will be kind and gentle, and that it will offer us good tidings all the time. This is the reason why so many people are frustrated and dejected. The wise have learned to accept the concept of Amor Fati—a concept that teaches us to accept all the sorts of things that life brings our way.

Even truly horrible things should be embraced and accepted. Then, a solution, if necessary, found. Embracing the really horrible things that life hands down to us is what stoics did. This includes accepting all the things, bad or good, that life hands you.

According to one popular stoic, we should not hope that all the things that we want in life will happen to us. Instead, we should ensure that we accept whatever life brings our way. This way, our lives will be more serene. And the Roman Emperor Marcus Aurelius was in complete agreement. He believed that whatever the world sends our way is fine with us. Nothing that comes our way at the right time is ever too early or too late. Being one with nature and accepting the things the world brings our way is one great way of being at peace and living a serene life.

How to live and accept Amor Fati

Plenty of people have a problem with Amor Fati. They do not believe that it is possible or easy just to accept the things life sends their way. After all, how do people just accept the horrible things that happen? Indeed, it can be quite challenging.

While Amor Fati did not actually originate from the stoics, the phrase originated from others. However, these two words and the meaning behind it sum up exactly what stoicism is all about. According to stoicism, Amor Fati is generally a mindset that is about accepting what life sends our way and folks should endeavor to make the best out of it.

It is advisable to be okay with the things that life throws our way and handling the things that come out rather than fighting them. Accepting the bad and good things and embracing them is how we should approach life.

When you apply the principle of Amor Fati, you are required to love these challenges and consider them essential parts of life. Amor Fati teaches us that all these things happen for a reason and it is up to us to turn these into positives.

In life, we are all embarking on a journey, and everyone's journey is unique. While it is advisable to accept fate and face the challenges that come about, others will find this difficult and unacceptable. For instance, there is parenthood and patriotism. With both these concepts, there will be tough times, including sacrifices and pain. However, these serve a great purpose, and in the end, there will be immense joy and fulfillment.

Life really should not be easy. We will get where we want to, but we have to begin where we are and face the circumstances that we are under. This is because life is not perfect and was never intended to be. We all have only one life, and it is possible to achieve something through it. However, we need to accept the fact that life is challenging and it can serve us plenty of unpleasant things along the way.

As such, we need to clearly understand the fact that it will not be "Christmas" every day. So, with all that said, how do we handle the bad situations? How are we supposed to react when we learn that we are not in charge of certain situations and will probably not attain all the things that we desire in life?

Avoid complaining and denial

There is an old saying that states, "Should you find yourself in a hole, stop digging." It is advisable not to deny reality but to accept and embrace it. It is only after you accept your situation and circumstances that you can do something about it. Also, complaining is never the solution. It is a complete waste of time and energy. This is often a sign that you are resisting a situation that you have no control over. Such energy and precious moments could be used to finding a lasting solution to the problem.

Human beings are by nature likely to complain, cry, sulk, and generally protest a bad situation. However, complaining and crying offer no solution and do not help to make things better. We all have a choice when faced with challenges; get furious and mad or pause and think about a solution. This begins with the acceptance of a situation and then moving ahead to fix the challenge.

We could be tempted to think that by accepting a bad situation we will not be able to find a solution and will therefore not accomplish anything. However, accepting a situation does not mean that you will not do anything about it. For instance, if you fall down the stairs and break your leg, you are not simply going to sit around and do nothing about it. You will definitely go to the hospital and seek medical help. However, stoicism requires you to accept the situation and think about a solution instead of expending energy worrying about things but without taking any action.

This is the same as being thrown in jail. If you are in jail, then you can choose to deny the fact that you are in jail or you could accept the fact and then do something about it. Being able to come around and accept the situation then come up with a pragmatic approach or solution to the problem is absolutely essential. This is, in most cases, perhaps the only solution available.

Look towards the future

When a bad incident happens, it often feels extremely painful at that moment. Sometimes it may feel like it is the end of the world. However, if you take a deep breath, pause for a moment, and think about the future, you will realize that things are not so bad.

Problems and challenges keep occurring all the time. Today's problem may seem like it is the worst while the next problem then seems worse than the one before it. And then again another problem will come, and it will seem even worse than all the others. It is much better to have a positive outlook no matter the challenges that come your way.

Whenever a disaster happens and challenges come our way, the best possible approach is to look into the future. Ideally, we should take the time to think about what the future holds and what we can do about our current circumstances in this regard. If we focus on the future, then the current problems and challenges will seem minute and trivial.

According to stoicism followers, we need to learn how to flash forward and look into the future. Thinking about the future even in the heat of present challenges makes them seem pretty trivial. In only a couple of months, or years (depending on the issue), you will not feel too bad about things. You will probably be elsewhere doing other things. This means you will be happier in the future after current troubles melt away.

View life like a game

Games are often challenging, and we all expect to be challenged regardless of the games we play. If you are playing a video game and manage to get to the second level, you will look forward to an even greater challenge than at the initial level. If there were no serious challenge, then you would probably be disappointed.

The same is true about life. Life will always have its challenges. Always look to the things within your control and handle them the best way possible rather than fret over things which you have no control over. This same principle applies to Special Forces training. Special operations forces like to view their training as a game and a special challenge, which they always look forward to conquering. If they viewed training as a make or break event, then they probably would not succeed.

Life is very similar to a game—we get in there and face the challenges it presents. Sometimes we try and fail. When this happens, then we should dust ourselves off and begin all over. Eventually, we will try and succeed. Failing can be frustrating, but it can also be fun. If you learn to welcome and embrace life's obstacles and hurdles, then you will definitely avoid frustrations and improve your chances of not just finding success but also happiness in life.

Learning to accept circumstances is an excellent way of overcoming difficult times, failures, and other life challenges. You should not complain or live in denial but always focus on the future, view life's challenges positively, and think about actions that can lead you towards the kind of success that you desire.

Be grateful for the positive and the challenges of life

Even as we agree that we should accept our current situations and focus on the future in order to strive, we still need to learn to love the truly horrible moments. As it is with most people, when bad things happen, we tend to believe that we are right and that the fault is not ours.

However, when we are in the moment, it is never easy to make a sober decision. You will not be able to arrive at the solution or have the answers that you need if you get into a tight spot. For instance, if you miss your flight, you will feel extremely disappointed. However, if the plane ends up crashing, then the incident of missing a flight will not be so disappointing after all.

Much of the time that people are ungrateful is when they view matters or issues without being objective. People tend to view issues from a subjective position, so they tend to be ungrateful. With objectivity, you will not be so sad or angry but will easily have gratitude for every situation. The most crucial aspect of gratitude is focusing on the future. If you pay close attention to the journey, then your burden will be lightened. You will be able to take on the future and the challenges that it brings forth. This way, you will be able to achieve happiness regardless of circumstances.

Amor Fati means to love fate

Since life dishes out lots of disappointments and challenges, rather than wish that things were different, it is better to embrace the challenges. This means not just accepting challenges but also embracing them. Embracing problems brought on by life is the ultimate source of strength and power. Weak individuals want things to be a certain way, but strong individuals muster the strength and embrace all their challenges and troubles.

To be successful, you should learn to embrace, accept, and even love challenges and misfortunes. In summary, the term Amor Fati simply teaches us to love every single bit of life including both good and bad times. Simply embracing or accepting it is not sufficient.

You should avoid denials as well as complaining. These two traits are your enemy as they will hinder you from making progress. No matter what happens to you, you should be able to overcome your difficulties and challenges. As such, the sooner you begin to accept yourself and your circumstances, the better it will be for you.

Always look forward into the future and do not dwell on present troubles. Your current problems will not bother you forever. Perhaps by the following month, you will have gotten over the challenges. As such, you should look forward and think about the best solution to your challenges and how to get to where you wish to be.

Learn to treat life as a game with challenges that keep getting tougher. If life is easy, then it is not fun. Some conflict here and there and some personal challenges always ensure that you emerge stronger and more successful. And lastly, you should have a grateful heart. No matter what happens to you always be grateful. You never know how the future will turn out, so embrace your current situation and be grateful about everything.

Stoicism is about doing things and not just reading

Stoicism is a practical kind of philosophy. It means people have to do things rather than just read about them. That is the reason why early stoics came up with practical ways of practicing stoicism. For instance, you cannot expect to read about martial arts and then go out there and perform like a pro. To be any good you will have to train hard and work hard for a long time.

This is why the early stoics came up with practical ways of living like a stoic. They did not just want people to read about stoicism but actually to practice it every day for true happiness. They came up with a number of exercises or rituals to be practiced. These are aimed at training the mind to respond appropriately to incidents and challenges that occur to us. This way, each time we can react appropriately.

Philosophers caution people not just to learn and understand things but also practice what they learn. This is because, with time, things tend to be forgotten and memories do fade. As such, we end up doing the opposite and practice things that are contrary to what we promote.

Over 2,000 years later, there is scientific evidence that shows that what the stoics determined back then is very true and accurate. Supposing you are feeling terrible because of the things life has handed you. What is your next course of action? As a stoic, there are a couple of things that you can do. Here are the practical things:

1. Ask yourself what you would recommend someone else do.

Let us assume you are riding with your friend and he or she is driving. There is traffic, so they blast the horn and stick their head out then yell at other motorists. You instead advise him or her to calm down and relax. The same incident happens the following day, but this time you are the driver. So will you act like your friend instinctively or will your actions be different?

This is a challenge that stoics noted many years ago. They knew that it was easy to ask others to act in a certain way, but it is harder to do the same. When it comes to us, we find it much harder to do the same. This is what Epictetus meant when he spoke of projective visualization.

Example: Let us take the example of a servant at our home. If the servant breaks a cup, we will be mad and furious at them, as the incident will disrupt our tranquility. However, to put this anger into perspective, think if this incident happened at a friend's house. We would probably not think much about it and would try to calm down our friend—telling them that it is only a cup that broke and that these things happen.

Projective visualization, according to Epictetus, is an excellent way of getting us to appreciate the kind of reaction we would have when things happen versus how we'd react when we are not directly affected. As such, we get to appreciate the insignificance of an incident that happens, and as such, will not allow it to interfere with our peace. Issues tend to be major and annoying when they happen to us but relatively insignificant when they occur to others.

In such matters, the principle of outside advice applies. This means asking yourself what you would do if recommending solutions to another person. In most cases, we would not think about our emotions and current state—

they would seem distant and removed. The bottom line in such cases is to simply do unto others what you would want them to do for you. This is akin to the Tonga rule which says, "Do unto yourself what you would recommend to others."

2. Apply the Assent Discipline.

You may begin to apply the Tonga rule in your life every single day. The stoics urged people not to get carried away by their feelings or thoughts. According to the discipline of assent, you should allow yourself to feel the desire and need to do something that you should not do, then avoid doing it completely.

This is a very difficult challenge, and most of us are unable to hold back. It only takes a very tiny moment to arrive at a decision but that moment is really the key. If you can manage that moment and do your very best to hold out each time, then it will eventually become a habit, and soon enough you will be avoiding anger and outbursts whenever something negative happens to you.

According to one of the early stoics, Epictetus, the key moment is to catch yourself when you are just about to react to a situation and then postpone the urge. All you need to do is hold your breath, pause, and think about your next course of action. Plenty of other philosophers have spoken about this moment as well. Basically, what this calls for is first catching yourself in the moment just before acting and then holding out rather than acting.

It is amazing if you manage to resist the impulse to act instantly after a horrible incident. However, is this something that you can repeatedly do? Can you manage to hold out long enough? Essentially, you will require a lot of willpower not to act but to hold out. Also, it is easier on the brain to postpone the act rather than put it off completely. This tactic works effectively.

According to philosophers, a habit really cannot be eradicated completely. Instead, it should be replaced by something else. To effectively change a habit, then we need to apply what is known as the golden rule of habit change. If we maintain the same impetus and reward, we can replace the current habit with a new one.

Getting rid of bad behavior is acceptable, but it is even better to replace it with good behavior. However, since human beings are always craving new and better things, we need always to maintain that craving. Because once it is done away with, humans will take things for granted. To maintain this kind of craving, the stoics offered a solution.

3. Turn these actions into a treat.

According to the stoics, runaway desire can turn you into a miserable person. In the words of Epictetus, a wise person is one who does not mourn the things he does not have but actually rejoices and celebrates the things he has. However, for stoics, they took things to the extreme.

For instance, they would get rid of things that they love and then start thinking about death and so on. They even deprived themselves of things that they liked and also ceased taking things for granted, such as health, friends, and so on. According to research, such actions do bear fruits. This kind of approach does work, and there is proof to that effect.

Example: Consider a section of the week when you are broke with very little food and dressed in shabby clothes. Then, ask yourself if this is really all that you fear. When you do this, you will find that it is actually not as bad as you think. However, you can get the same results through less strenuous ways.

Think about all the things that you used to cherish that you nowadays take for granted. For instance, think about the morning coffee that used to feel really great but now you down it without a glimmer of gratitude. Now avoid this coffee for three or four days and see how that goes. According to philosophers, this is an excellent way of beginning to appreciate, yet again, many of the things that you take for granted today.

Basically, if you enjoy your morning cup of coffee, simply skip it for a couple of days. When you have the coffee again, it will taste a lot better and will be way more amazing. The trick here is not to give up something completely but to set it aside for a couple of days.

The stoics want you to enjoy your coffee and generally enjoy life and all it has to offer. All they avoided were negative emotions, but they were emotional beings, and they embraced all their emotions. They also believed that people should focus on the present and savor what is right in front of them rather than focus on an uncertain future. When the soul is anxious about future events, no longer will a person suffer from misery but anxiety. The soul may never enjoy rest if it focuses on things to come rather than the things at hand.

Science also supports the stoics because when you focus on the future, you are unable to enjoy the present. You will be happier if you focus your energy on the joyous experiences at hand. The most crucial ingredient for savoring the present is focused attention. You should find the time and make an effort to celebrate the positive. This way, you will enrich your life and enjoy quality wellbeing.

4. Learn always to review your day.

The stoics emphasized the need to review each day to provide insights on improving your life. Every single day should be up for review. By looking back on your day and reflecting upon it, you increase your chances of having a better day the following day and a more peaceful and tranquil future.

Before bowing down and sleeping, examine your day and ask what it is that you did wrong and what things you did not do that you should have done. This way, you will be able to take note and improve your tomorrow. Even then, you should be like Seneca and have compassion for yourself. Self-compassion is advised, so forgive yourself and identify areas where you could do with some improvement.

Chapter 2: Power of Stoicism Philosophy For a Better Life

Stoicism is an ancient philosophy whose application is very relevant to modern-day living. Many people are beginning to show interest in this philosophy and wish to learn more about it and apply it to their lives. Some of the early stoics such as Seneca the Younger and Marcus Aurelia were great thinkers and philosophers. Some of their writings have turned out to be best sellers.

Many people today are buying stoicism literature including self-help books based on the works of early stoics such as Epictetus and Marcus Aurelius. It is best to view stoicism just as the early stoics intended it.

Stoicism is basically a system of thought

While stoicism insists on action to apply its principles, it includes much more than just an ethical philosophy. At its core are a system of logic, a theory of reality, physics, and the vastness of the universe. The most basic aspect of stoicism calls on not taking anything in life for granted.

Stoicism consists of embracing contemplation. This embrace of contemplation is very similar to numerous other philosophies and schools of thought. Stoicism teaches us that to lead fulfilling lives we need to ask ourselves tough questions. We need to ask ourselves what it is like to be human and how we react when visited by misfortune or challenges. According to the ancient stoics, the best solution is to reason things out and think things over before acting. And reason definitely needs a disciplined mind.

According to great thinkers and philosophers, philosophy is the endeavor to answer the question "How should I live?" To respond appropriately to this question posed by philosophy, we need to have a reasonable understanding of the world that we live in as well as our relationship with it.

As such, philosophy is not really about finding the truth about life but more about finding traction to walk steadily even as others around you slip and fall by the wayside. If you get to know and appreciate your place in the universe, then you will easily be able to make considerations on the way you should live so that you can live life in tandem with the values that you hold dear and those which you set up for yourself.

Stoicism philosophy

Stoicism, as we have already determined, is a school of philosophy from Ancient Greece that was founded by Zeno of Citium in the city of Athens. According to this school of philosophy, virtue is the highest form of good and is based on knowledge. Wise people exist in tandem with providence and fate that govern nature. They are also unbothered by the outcomes of good fortune and indifferent to pain and pleasure.

Stoicism can also be viewed as the things in life that occur to us and our reactions to them. As such, it is crucial to separate matters within our control, such as thoughts and emotions, from all those issues that are beyond our control. To view things with the right perspective, we need to be able to control our thoughts and emotions.

If you can control your thoughts and emotions, then you can view the honest truth in different things and situations. Think about a bottle of soda. The soda is neither good nor bad. It just exists. Now, if you drink the soda, you will enjoy the nice and sweet taste. However, soda adds no nutritional value to you and will only cause you to gain weight and probably raise your blood sugar levels.

Now if you know this truth, you can view the soda differently based on how you choose to. If you love the soft drink and enjoy its fizzy and sugary taste, then you will more likely focus on the positives and ignore any negatives. On the other hand, if you are health conscious and focused on your personal health, you will want to stay as far away from the soda as possible. Your reactions to the soda, drawing you towards or away from it, are guided by your emotions.

The emotions guiding you are definitely found within you. This means you can influence and control them even though sometimes this is not an easy thing to do. If you can take charge of your emotions, then you can always choose if and when to drink a soda and when not to. This, in the end, becomes a cost versus benefit matter where you consider your actions, which consequently determine the outcome.

This kind of perspective can now be applied to numerous other instances in your life. If you keep taking this kind of perspective in life, then you will make it a habit. You will basically train your mind to seek knowledge about a certain issue, about what the consequences or outcomes of an incident are, and then make decisions based on this knowledge.

The realization that our emotions and desires have a powerful effect on the things that we choose to do and those we choose not to do is a powerful one. They often tend to lead us towards plenty of things that are detrimental to our lives and with no real benefit to us. Our desires and emotions lead us to experiences that, in the end, have terrible outcomes. It also may happen that our emotions and desires may guide us away from positive experiences that will impact us in numerous great ways.

Also, when you know your place in the world, and know yourself pretty well, it will enable you to think about the best way to live so that you always abide by the set of values you want for yourself. As it is, you should never be too busy in life such that you lack the time necessary to focus on your life.

Stoicism and meditation

According to philosophers, a man who is too busy to meditate for ten minutes each day should actually meditate for an entire hour every day. Much of what most people know regarding meditation is obtained from the meditations of Marcus Aurelius himself. He became the emperor of Rome at a tender age and was at war throughout his reign. While he always emerged victorious in his wars against other empires and northern tribes, they took a huge toll on him. As such, he decided to spend his time in his thoughts.

He began meditating and thinking about different things and issues. He found solace within his thoughts just like all stoics are supposed to. He began to record and write about his meditation, and it was meant to be private.

He did not write from a philosophical point of view at all and did not quote other philosophers and thinkers. His writings were therefore mostly about his own philosophical thoughts and meditations.

The stoic philosophy of Marcus Aurelius

Here is a brief look at some of the quotations and philosophies of Marcus Aurelius. They are delivered from a stoicism perspective in order to understand the basic yet crucial aspects of stoicism.

According to Marcus, all things are linked together, and this togetherness is sacred. This thought originates from 'monism' which is ancient philosophy. According to this ancient philosophy, the universe is inherently one.

Stoics strongly believed in God. They believed that God is the single entity that brings together all substances together. Think about entities such as water, fire, and earth. The ultimate substance that unites all of these entities is God himself. And since God Almighty is supreme, we should always endeavor to work in tandem with nature in order to be closer to God.

Marcus also stated that everything that occurs happens for a reason. And if you do observe closely, you will very likely get to see it that way. According to this philosophy, the entire universe is united as one even though there are certain different entities. If everything is united in some way, then it is possible that all things work together in tandem. And if all things are perfect, then there is no other way. According to the stoics, all events that do occur are actually predetermined. In philosophy, this phenomenon is known as 'determinism'.

Stoics believe that we have power over our minds, but we have zero power over events. As an individual, you possess power over your mind but not over events beyond you. Due to this fact, you cannot do anything to affect the course of events. You can control your thought process as well as emotions. As such, when events occur, we can only control our reactions to them.

To lead a tranquil and happy life, we should learn to control our emotions when things do not go according to our wishes. Finding the mental strength necessary to achieve this is what stoicism philosophy puts forth. Stoics are well known for their mental strength. When tragedy visits, they can handle it with dignity and calm.

There is a huge difference between stoics and ordinary people. The ordinary person may pray not to go through a misfortune; however, the stoic will pray for strength to handle the misfortune. Think about Marcus who lost two infant kids at one point in his life. When the misfortune happened, his thoughts were that it was okay, but he prayed to have the strength necessary to overcome such a challenge.

Many years ago, perhaps even decades ago, the British taught stoicism in school. It is thought to be the reason behind the stiff upper lip they are often accused of. This, however, emanates from the stiff faces they wear when tragedy and misfortunes visit.

Any impediments that hinder action actually advance action. Anything that blocks the way turns out to be the way. As we noted earlier, everything in the universe is predetermined, and nothing simply happens. Because of this principle, there is nothing that you can do about your circumstances, but you can control how you react to these circumstances.

According to the stoics, there is no single truth because all that we hear is not fact but simply opinion. As such, all that we see can be termed as a perspective and not the truth. Human beings are a tiny fragment of the universe which is a true and perfect entity.

Since humans are a fragment of the universe, they cannot truly get to know everything. According to Emperor Marcus Aurelius, we need to practice what is known as 'perspectivism'. Perspectivism is an ancient philosophy where the notion that any human can access the ultimate truth is rejected. It is different from relativism which observes no truth at all in the world.

Perspectivism accepts the idea of truth only in that human understanding of the same is flawed and mediated which hinders our complete access of the truth. Each individual has an opinion which cannot be discounted. This opinion, therefore, is simply a perspective which could be closer or further from the truth but definitely not the absolute truth.

Also, according to Marcus, there is no infallible person because the infallible human being does not exist. It is impossible to definitively judge an individual as there is no absolute truth but only perspectives which could be closer or further from the truth. Stoicism is not a panacea for all the information and does not promise or offer perfect knowledge. Nature is generally governed by reason yet there is an authority that is higher than reason. Because of this reason, there is no human being that can claim infallibility. This showcases the differences between wisdom and intelligence. Wise people can tell the limitations of their intelligence.

Virtue should be visible in your actions and not simply in theory

According to philosophers, we need good and virtuous character if we are to conduct ourselves diligently. Diligent actions emanate from virtuous persons. Therefore, instead of wasting time debating the virtues of a good person, we should strive to become one. So always strive to be a person of virtue because they say that virtue resides in a person of good character.

Stoics and philosophers teach us that we are what we think we are. According to the thoughts of Emperor Marcus, what you think about will eventually determine the content or quality of what is on your mind. And our thoughts eventually reflect on our soul, and this also shows on our faces and demeanor.

Our conduct principally emanates from reason and thought. Our emotions betray our judgments and as such are deemed cognitive. Take the emotion of greed for instance. Greed constitutes a fallacy in judgment as people get the wrong impression on the intrinsic value of possessions and money. Stoics always endeavor to exist in tandem with nature, and as such, they treasure reason. The reason is held in high regard above everything else because the entire universe is overseen and maintained by the law of reason.

Our lives have eternal meaning as our actions ripple into eternity. The stoics strongly believe that the universe is eternal and it constitutes God. God is perfect and true and eternal, and basically, anything perfect is eternal. Human beings are part of the wider universe, and all the things that we do in this life constitute a portion of the universe.

It is common for people to speak of the enormous expanse of the universe in relation to how minute human beings are. However, what such folks do not take into account is infinity. Since the universe is infinite, then our activities and thoughts are extremely important as they constitute that infinite universe.

If you want to lead a happy life that is content and tranquil, then you should ensure that you think only quality thoughts. The world that we live in is quite complex, and so are we. As such, if we contemplate and improve the quality of our thought process, then we will get rid of confused thinking, spiritual exhaustion, and emotional problems. However, contemplating does take effort and courage. If you are courageous, then find the time and organize your thoughts. And if you have time, then you should find the courage. If you do, you can align your thought process.

Lead a better life with stoicism principles

As human beings, we have emotions. We can control these emotions even though it is not an easy thing to do. Think about the innocent bottle of soda which is neither good nor bad. You know that if you drink the soda, you will enjoy the fizzy drink and sweet taste and probably feel refreshed. However, sodas can spike up your blood sugar levels and add hundreds of calories to your body. You will be exposed to lifestyle diseases like diabetes, and probably gain weight. As such, you will enjoy the soda for a couple of minutes, but the problems will follow you for a long time.

Taking perspective when thinking about issues and events is crucial and will determine how you will lead your life. By taking perspective and thinking about consequences, you will start doing this in all aspects and at all times. It will eventually dawn on you that desires and emotions point you in the direction where your life will not benefit and instead will suffer consequences. If you follow emotions as well as desires, you will experience major negatives in your life, and you will also be directed away from things that are good for your life.

There are stoicism principles that can guide your life in the right direction. The important ones are only a couple and are very straightforward. However, they contain lots of great ideas, much of which are applicable in our lives. Your life does not have to be strictly stoic, but you can adapt some of these principles to lead a better, more tranquil and more fulfilling life. Let us examine a couple of these principles:

1. We create our feelings, and our emotions originate from within

As a human being and an individual, you have the sole responsibility to determine if you like someone or want something. The decisions that you make about what you love, want, or like are entirely up to you. However, the situation is rather different as most people react automatically to situations and never pause to think that the solution should come from within.

Take a moment to consider the feeling you get when you receive a plate of your favorite meal. Perhaps the feeling compares closely to seeing your favorite person or close friend. The feeling is perhaps great. However, you are the source of feelings and emotions. These emanate from deep within you. They are authentic feelings because they come from within, are a natural response, and are your creation.

You get similar feelings when it comes to buying something new. Being in charge of your emotions and feelings is crucial. If you want to be successful professionally, personally, and financially, then you need to create the correct emotional response, which in most cases is usually the correct one.

2. Work closely with a respected mentor

We often make decisions in life based on our understanding and knowledge of the world that we live in. With time, the experiences that we gain through life get to teach us a lot and open our eyes to plenty of things. However, when we are young, we lack experience and exposure.

This is why it is advisable to work with a mentor. A good mentor will walk you through some of life's challenges and situations. We have different kinds of mentors including life mentors, professional mentors, and so on. They are all crucial and can help in numerous ways.

There are all kinds of mentors that you could choose ranging from pastors to experienced business executives or even a trusted relative. A professional mentor can help with career or business advice, while a trusted life mentor can be any trusted person in the community.

There is a reason why mentors are necessary—they play a crucial role in mentoring people and guiding them in making important decisions without involving personal emotions. When a mentor is helping you make a decision, he or she will usually have your best interest at heart as they have no personal attachment or emotional stake.

A mentor will walk you through your options and then enlighten and educate you about each option. That way, you can make enlightened decisions rather than emotional or uneducated ones. This can prove invaluable rather than simply making judgments clouded in emotion.

3. Failures will occur, but life must go on

Fear is a powerful emotion and among the most powerful. People are generally afraid of many things. These include missing out on important things, losing a relationship, contracting a major disease, hurting their careers, and so on. There is a great fear of failure, and people view it as a hugely negative thing.

However, fear is simply an emotion like all other emotions. The challenge with this emotion is that it discourages us from taking risks and also urges us to avoid risking failure regardless of any possible outcomes. If we can challenge fear, then we can undertake a lot more risks, and this will open us up to more opportunities. Being afraid of taking risks because of the fear of failure does hold back many people who would otherwise have been extremely successful.

It would be extremely unfortunate for anyone to lose out on an opportunity simply because of fear. As it is, fear should never hold back any individual from putting themselves out there fully. Should there be an opportunity available to you, then the best course of action is to analyze it and observe whether there are any chances of success and what possibilities for failure exist.

The best approach to conquering fear is facing the facts head on. You also need to analyze your chances of success and whether you are capable of handling defeat or any losses. Basically, you only need a reasonable opportunity to weigh the possible benefits versus losses or risks.

Fear is generally an emotion that can hold you back. However, if you realize that it is only an emotion just like any other, then you will be willing to take on more risks and consider all the financial, personal and professional risks available to you.

4. Read and learn, then apply the knowledge that you acquire

As a stoic, you need to acquire knowledge but apply it practically. Stoicism requires that we learn how to evaluate situations, things, places, and people. When you do the evaluation, you should never let your emotions interfere. Instead, you should use your knowledge and mind to analyze people, situations, and things in order to get the best outcome.

If you wish to become a better person in numerous ways, then you should increase your knowledge, evaluate your words, and then apply the knowledge that you acquire. If you apply that knowledge appropriately to this world, then you will become a better person with a strong character and will live a fulfilling and successful life.

Sometimes uncertainty and situations of fear may arise. This is because every opportunity in life comes with a certain risk of failure and this is deemed okay. When we fail, it is never the end of the world; in fact, failure can be considered a positive thing because we are likely to learn valuable lessons from it. You should never allow the fear of failure to hold you back and deny you a fair chance at progressing in life or achieving something.

5. Always be brutally honest with yourself

One of the best gifts that we can give ourselves is honesty. You should not hold extremely high standards of yourself such that you have to be dishonest sometimes. In this world, there is no perfect individual. However, it is common to find people holding highly inflated views of themselves. If you have an inflated view of yourself, then you risk falling behind others. Should this happen, you will be forced into a situation where you have to be dishonest just to maintain an above-average persona.

Should this be the case, then you will put yourself at risk regarding missing out on numerous opportunities including those in your relationships, career, finances, and so on. Problems and issues will then occur, such as jealousy, anger, and rejection. These and many other negative reactions will ensue when you are not honest with yourself.

One of the most important things that you need to do is to be absolutely honest with yourself. You need to face up to some honesty and be true to yourself. For instance, if it is your skills or experience, you need to own your levels. Determine the areas where you are skilled or have sufficient experience and highlight these. Also, ensure that you note areas that need improvement. Remember that you do not necessarily need to be brutally honest with others but only with yourself. Being brutally honest with others is sometimes considered cruel. Plenty of people will dislike you and avoid you like the plague. Treat others politely and only be brutally honest with yourself.

6. Always reflect on your time usage

Self-improvement and self-reliance are among the tenets that stoicism identifies with. As an individual looking to adopt the stoic kind of lifestyle, you need to be able to detach yourself completely from your emotions and view the world in its empirical or most basic form.

Accept your position wherever you may be in life and then choose to ramp it up from there. If you take note of your attributes and seek to get better or apply yourself the best way possible, then you will be much happier and successful. The reason why is that you will seek to acquire as much information as possible and also seek to improve your personal traits and physical wellbeing.

One main challenge that most people encounter when trying to better themselves is finding the time. We are almost unable to find time to study and improve our skills and widen our knowledge. People cannot even find time to go to the gym and work out just to be fit, possibly develop some muscle, and lose weight. As it is, time management is a tough challenge for most people. If you can properly manage your time, you can accomplish all that you want and find the time to increase your knowledge and work out in order to be fit and healthy.

The best approach to doing this is to start a diary. Others include digital time trackers found on Smartphones and computers. A time tracker will help you to keep track of your time all day. This way, you can take note of sections of the day where you can find or save time to do other things.

7. Think about how you spend your money

Everything mentioned above regarding time management also applies to money. Many of us earn plenty of money but are unsure of how it is spent. It is amazing, though, that people who earn relatively less amounts are actually able to do much more with it. And those who earn relatively large amounts are likely to spend it on things that are not necessary. Learning how to be prudent with your money will enable you to achieve more and perform better in various ways.

First of all, you need to take a closer look at how you spend your money. Think about what is important and what is not regarding your personal expenditure. The best way to do this is to budget your money or use a spending tracker. A good budget is ideal because it allows you to plan and allocate money to each sector of your life that you deem crucial.

If you budget your money appropriately, you can note where you overspend and where it is that you can make savings. If you are wasting any money, then the spending tracker or budget will point this out for you.

8. Think about your purpose in life and are you on track with that purpose

Everyone has a purpose in life. We are all born to achieve something crucial. However, just thinking about one's purpose can be rather tasking and most people cannot explain clearly their purpose. It is important to think about our purpose in life and how we live our lives in line with this purpose.

All in all, you will find it extremely fulfilling if you spend your time and money on something that you love. Many people claim that they feel very fulfilled when they spend their effort, time, energy, and money on causes that they strongly believe in. Also, people tend to feel bad and sometimes guilty when they spend their energy, time, and money on things that are not in line with their purpose in life. As such, you should focus on using purpose as a guide to how to spend your money as well as most other things that you possess.

9. Avoid procrastination at all costs

One of the worst things to do is to procrastinate. Unfortunately, we all too often tend to procrastinate believing we can put aside issues and deal with them later. The early stoics strongly believed in saving time and good time management. The reason is that any time that you waste will never be recovered. As they say, time and tide truly await no one.

Also, when you procrastinate, you tend to spend time on things, matters, issues, and problems that are not aligned to your purpose in life. As such, you waste so much time on things that probably do not add much value to your life. Think about the things that are important to you. Focus on these things and put more time and effort into them.

When you write down the things that are important to you, then align them with your purpose in life, you will find that you procrastinate less and focus more on what is truly important. Basically, many people will find that time management is a crucial area of their lives where they need to improve.

10. Be present in each moment

We have learned that stoicism heavily relies on things such as self-improvement and self-reliance. We often let our instincts take the lead rather than reason. When we space out of a situation, we rely on instinct, and instincts rely on emotion. Because of relying on emotion, our reactions tend to be irrational. We can perform better and be more successful when we are present in each moment. This means that we can receive more from any situation as well as make more informed decisions when we allow ourselves to be present in the moment. Therefore, try and ensure that you are present in each moment so that you perform better and have a more positive outcome.

Chapter 3: Learn How to Overcome Self-doubt, Self-Criticism, and Feelings of Inadequacy

According to Seneca, one of the early stoics, humans are usually more frightened than hurt. He also said that humans are in anguish more because of their imagination rather than real happenings.

As a person, you are probably suffering from fear of rejection and even feelings of inadequacy. Maybe you feel like you are not good enough. There are numerous causes of this. For instance, you could feel all your mistakes playing out right in front of you. Sometimes your self-esteem may tank, and your confidence tumbles to the ground.

Fortunately, you are not alone, and this is not an isolated issue. Many people constantly feel inadequate; it is a phenomenon that has been occurring from the onset of human life. This old problem also has an old solution, and the old solution works perfectly.

Our feelings emanate from our thoughts

According to stoics, the bad things that happen to us do not necessarily cause us to be sad. Our sadness does not emanate from the rock that breaks your window or from the rude pedestrian on the street. Our emotional reactions are as a result of our beliefs, judgments, and thoughts.

Stoics such as Epictetus clearly stated that it is not events that generally bother people, but it is how people perceive them. And this is what forms the basis of what is now referred to as 'Cognitive Behavioral Therapy'.

Cognitive Behavioral Therapy (CGT)

Cognitive behavioral therapy operates on the concept that our thoughts greatly affect our feelings which in turn affect our actions. In the end, our actions end up influencing our results and circumstances in life.

As it is, the different situations and incidents that we encounter in life do not necessarily affect our feelings. What does is our interpretation of things or how we see things and even the words that people speak that tend to affect our feelings. Many people doubt this theory and believe that people's words and thoughts affect them directly.

Let's say that you draw something from your pocket that resembles a weapon. If you point it at another person and they believe it is a water pistol, then they will not be affected. However, if they believe that the gun-like thing pointed towards them is a weapon, then they will react differently. Your behavior will remain the same, but it is their perception of it that changes. Therefore, their thoughts will affect their reaction.

As it is, beliefs do not really matter when it comes to our actions. The thought process is really key here. If you can work on your thoughts, then your actions will be completely different. This is something that stoics realize. They understand that humans need to ask questions relating to unhelpful and irrational beliefs, so we lead more productive and helpful lives. It is our beliefs that drive our reactions and feelings.

Stoics also determine that human beings are prone to asking questions especially of beliefs that are unhelpful or irrational. However, even as we eliminate negative and irrational thoughts from our minds, we do not necessarily have to replace these with positive ones. Instead, we need to find rational affirmations and useful thoughts. Here is how to go about this challenge:

1. Seek out and identify misguided thoughts

There is often a voice in our heads whispering thoughts that lower our self-esteem and get us to lose confidence. Sometimes we feel uncomfortable for one reason or another. It is good to ask ourselves what the problem is that is causing us to lose confidence.

The first instance is to think what thoughts are on your mind. It could be something like, "You are such a failure," or "What an idiot." Now that the thoughts have been identified, the next step is to challenge these thoughts. You need to pause and interrogate the thoughts. According to Epictetus, you need to put the thoughts to the test to find out their origin or cause.

Cognitive behavioral therapy offers a solution for these misguided thoughts. Distorted thoughts should always attract a rational response. A distorted thought could tell you that you are useless and will never amount to anything if you mess up. You will think that you are a total failure and that nothing in your life will ever work out. These are irrational and distorted thoughts that are untrue and without a basis.

Rational thoughts, on the other hand, will come up with a reasonable response. For instance, if you mess up a project, the rational thought will speak sense. It will let you know that you have probably accomplished such projects before and are therefore not a failure. Also, you may have failed this time, but you will most likely succeed next time.

You should never allow the overreaching, negative, and upsetting thoughts to get past without being challenged. As soon as such thoughts make an appearance, you should pause and challenge them to correct them and set out a legitimate thought process. If you keep doing this, then you will make it a habit and will eventually learn how to get rid of all irrational thoughts instinctively. This works well for those with negative thoughts. However, there are others who have low self-esteem and suffer from a lack of confidence—this is viewed differently.

2. Examine your core beliefs

Many people occasionally feel down and low, and this may not necessarily be caused by occasional negative thoughts. Sometimes it is our system of core beliefs. Some of these beliefs could be negative. Some people think that they are not beautiful or desirable and no one can love them. Others believe that they are losers who will never amount to anything useful. Thus, this all boils down to a person's core beliefs.

If you have such beliefs within you, then challenging them could prove to be a daunting task. Such concepts are often ingrained into our minds that it becomes quite a challenge to confront them. While it could pose a daunting challenge, there are a couple of things we can do instead.

Our belief systems are set up so that a person notices factors that promote negative thoughts rather than those promoting the positive ones. As such, it becomes quite difficult to challenge them. This is why low self-esteem is a bigger trial compared to irrational thoughts.

Evidence that supports positive thoughts is also always just a little more difficult to present. One way of revealing this kind of positive evidence is to examine our past experiences in order to identify this evidence which promotes our healthy beliefs. Another helper that will provide evidence in support of positive thoughts is proper counsel.

This counsel that you need is the close friend or family member that constantly reminds you of all your positive attributes. Such a person regularly reinforces the great things you have achieved and your potential to achieve even more. You close friend will constantly mention how valuable and important you are. This kind of reinforcement will put forth evidence that you need to counter the negative evidence presented by the negative thoughts and low self-esteem.

It is advisable to hang around friends who were present when you exhibited your strengths and showcased your strong points. Friends could remind you of those moments with lots of conviction because they were present at the time. Putting these strengths down on paper and having a credible list is extremely crucial to overcoming your low self-esteem issues. You will have an accurate and rational list to follow, and this will definitely boost your confidence.

Even after addressing your core beliefs, things will not change instantly. According to the stoics, it is important to take some time each day and reflect on the day's events to keep getting better. According to Seneca, you need to keep a regular watch over yourself and review each day. We need to edit and balance the happenings of every single day.

3. Review the events of each day

Now when your thoughts say that you are a loser, you will counter them with evidence that you are actually strong and capable. However, this should not be an event but a process undertaken often and most possibly every day. In the meantime, you need to continue keeping a record of your strengths and successes.

A regular log of evidence that keeps increasing constitutes a powerful tool that you can use to develop positive beliefs. This way, you will become less reactive to incidents that pull you down. The evidence log is, therefore, a power that can help you overcome some of the challenges posed by low self-esteem. The stoics recommend the development of this powerful tool in conjunction with a daily review of the events that you encounter.

In due course, you will eventually begin seeing positives in your life. You will also get to notice positive attributes and eventually begin to associate with them. This regular association with your strengths will improve and boost your self-esteem and instill more positive thoughts.

4. Get a cognitive cue card

There are the ABCs of positivity. Always Be Challenging. You need to always monitor any negative thoughts within your mind. These thoughts need to be checked and challenged regularly. Anytime an external stimulus disturbs your peace, remember that it is not the external stimulus that bothers you but your thoughts about it. It is possible to wipe out these thoughts in a matter of minutes—according to Emperor Marcus.

The best approach to changing your thought process is to make it as smooth and easy as possible. This way, you will avoid regularly arguing with, or focusing too much on, your time and energy. As such, you will need to prepare and have ready a complete list of positive thoughts or responses to counter any negative thoughts that may play in your mind.

Should you feel exhausted without the energy to battle negative thoughts or low self-esteem, then the best approach to use is the cue card. A cognitive cue card is a tool that can accurately enable you to interpret negative thoughts in a positive way. Rational thoughts will help you counter the negative thoughts, and with time, it will become normal.

These are real and actual cards designed to be tools that help you to perform better. Using these cards will enable you to perform better and calm you down. All you have to do is to write a card detailing your beliefs and the kind of positive message with attributes that you would like to hear. Structuring the cards is easy. They could say things like, *just because I didn't succeed today, doesn't mean I will not succeed tomorrow.* Or maybe, *just because I am short, doesn't mean that I will not achieve much.*

Keep this kind of energy up. You may want to spin a positive angle to it. For instance, you could say, *I may have failed yesterday, but today I will emerge a winner.* Maintain this kind of momentum and ensure that you keep going each day until positive thoughts become second nature to you.

Summary

In short, it is important first to note and then confront any distorted and negative thoughts in your mind. The next approach is to focus on your core beliefs and put them to the test. This is crucial if you are to change your way of thinking. After this, you will need to come up with a positive thought that will counter any negatives. Also, review your day every evening and take notes appropriately. Finally, have cognitive cue cards to revamp positivity both in your mind and life.

Chapter 4: Five Actionable Mind Training Strategies to Eliminate Self-Defeating Thoughts

When you take a look at successful individuals, you will notice a couple of standout factors. First is that they all possess certain qualities such as passion, expertise, understanding, and grit. However, there are certain things that we may not see. Successful and peaceful people often have certain inner qualities that are not visible, including the inner system within an individual.

Each individual has a philosophy or a set of values they hold dear—at least most happy and successful individuals do. Such individuals follow a set of principles that guide their behavior and mind. However, what happens when failure ensues? How are we supposed to respond where there is an adverse situation?

Stoicism philosophy

Philosophy teaches us how to become better people and how to lead better lives. The stoic philosophy helps us to overcome tribulations and trials that life brings our way.

There are some complex and abstract philosophies out there, but stoicism is simple and easy to follow. It provides us with the skills, tools, and knowledge necessary to overcome life's challenges and to enable us to achieve our endeavors.

Stoicism provides a practical set of rules for all people, especially artists, writers, and even entrepreneurs. The main focus on stoics' philosophy is to guide people on how to become better people and how to lead happy and more satisfying lives. The philosophy aims at guiding people to gain peace within as they face and conquer life's challenges.

Stoicism is a philosophy that guides us to overcome adversity through tenets such as self-control, coming into touch with our nature, awareness of feelings and reactions, and the minimal time that we have. Stoics actually lived these principles via regular meditations, so they were always one with nature but never against it. We all face numerous challenges in life so we need to be cognizant of this fact and understand the nature of these challenges.

We should not run away from our problems and challenges; we should be ready to understand the adversities so we can react appropriately to them. It is advisable to understand how to transform adversity into food that feeds the hunger in us. Some of the principles from the early stoics will promote better work, boost your creativity, improve your life, and raise your general state of mind.

As a creative, you need to be adaptive, committed, vulnerable, and full of courage. To achieve this, you need to have a mind that is focused and can easily handle and alter any adversities, distractions, and negative thoughts. Instead, stoicism principles require that we pay more attention to our minds and hearts and focus on the important things. This can be a little difficult to attain though.

To be successful, you need to adopt a philosophy that is effective and proven to work. A good philosophy is one that works for you and helps to protect you from your weaknesses. Furthermore, you will not fall to distractions or excuses. Without principle, we will often succumb to our emotions rather than principle. However, when we are guided by principle in our work, careers, and life, then we will emerge more successful and perform well at anything we set our minds to. Here are some tips on how to apply stoicism principles and philosophy into your life:

1. First, accept that emotions develop from within

According to Marcus Aurelius, it is possible to get rid of anxiety or even discard it because it is within us and in our perceptions but from without. External stimuli cannot make us feel horrible on the inside. It is more of the things that we keep telling ourselves that will stress us out. Basically, you cannot be hurt or damaged by a plain document or canvas. These are never stressful. The stress emanates from the thoughts within you.

Much of the time we want to blame external forces or others for our feelings. However, all our feelings emanate from the inside. We create our feelings based on our perception of events. Essentially your mind is like a blank canvas or plain document. Such a piece cannot be stressful as such—your stresses will only come from within.

Most of the time we want to blame others for our feelings. This is because it is an easy thing to do and is the path of least resistance. However, it is important that we accept the truth which is that all conflict begins within us. It all begins in our minds. Ideally, when we run away from our responsibilities, then we are causing harm to ourselves. We also pay no heed to discipline which is absolutely important.

Should some hindrance or challenge come your way, then you should not blame external factors. Instead, you should look within and find a solution from the inside. As the stoics said, we are not so much disturbed by the things that happen to us but rather the things we tell ourselves.

2. Identify an honest person, then use them to remain honest

Find someone whose persona, actions, and life mirror his or her character and are generally acceptable to you and others. Such a person of high moral and character can act as a pillar in your life and will help you to keep things real. You need to keep looking up to this individual as a role model and guardian. This is crucial especially for individuals whose character is exceptional and is accepted by society and across the board. In order to straighten your act and become a much better person, you will need a mirror or ruler to measure against.

We all do plenty of things in the course of our lives. For instance, some people write books, write blogs, paint portraits, draw cartoons, and even create application programs. In all these different aspects, you need to ensure that there is a respected person that you can look up to. You need to learn from such a person and this you can do through examining their techniques, skills, works, stories, and even their successes and failures.

Also, you should take the time to read the works of your chosen person, listen to their interviews, and sometimes even write an email to them requesting some advice, tips, and so on. This will enable you to chart a pathway to success which you can then use for your benefit.

One of the most important things that you need to note is that you should not use this to compare yourself with your preferred role models. For instance, if you do not attain success after a week, like one of your role models or do not find love after three months like your other role model, it does not mean that you have failed. However, you can learn from successful individuals such as your heroes. These heroes and role models have principles and teachings, and just about every successful individual has a role model that they look up to, so having one is a sign of strength and never one of weakness.

3. There is life and opportunity after failure

For many people, a major incident, especially failure, hinders them from acting with sanity, self-control, justice, humility, honesty, and within reason. As such, they cannot fulfill their purposes, desires, ambitions, and so on. This is a wrong and definitely disastrous path to take. It is crucial to note that whenever something threatens to cause you pain, the thing itself is not the issue; you can avoid the pain and still prevail by organizing your thought process.

As an example, you can spend much of your time, resources, and effort working on a project for a whole year only to have others criticize it, ridicule your work and even outright ignore it. This can happen, and others will not necessarily appreciate your work.

Failure can seem exactly like this. However, recovering from a tragic incident like this is important, necessary, and crucial. You need to have the right mindset as well as practice it whenever it happens, so you master the skills. If you learn any lesson from this, it should be that you will now be able to work better. Basically, you will not experience growth without some measure of failure.

4. Read widely and with a purpose then apply the knowledge

While reading books is vital, just reading does not add value to your life. What is even more imperative is being able to apply the knowledge obtained from reading the books. The mind needs training, and books constitute the training props and weights necessary. Books on their own do not add much value to our lives; it is the knowledge, skills, and wisdom we obtain from them and how we apply such things to our lives that matters.

A person can read excellent books on business, marketing, management, and so on. They will learn a great deal through studying and will become extremely aware. When you read widely and study thoroughly, then you prepare your mind to do even greater things. You will avoid making silly mistakes and foolish errors. Even then, any failure should be considered as an advantage because it is a prelude to better and more success.

We obtain an education to acquire knowledge and internalize it. However, of more importance is ensuring that the education we obtain enables us to make wiser decisions and also to get us to act appropriately. Many people also read self-help books, which makes them feel happy in the moment. However, you will still need to calm and maintain your principles even when you have a rude customer, a troll, or an angry person screaming at you.

5. Ensure that you are brutally honest with yourself

If you need to save yourself, then the thing you need to do is always be conscious of any ills and wrongs that you commit. Basically, anyone who commits an evil act or engages in wrongdoing, but is unaware of it, will see no need to make things right. If you are to reform your habits, then you need to be aware of the ills that you commit.

Some people are proud of their wrong and evil deeds— this is not the way to go. The best approach is to feel guilty about your wrong actions and demonstrate this guilt. Also, you should go ahead and engage in some inquiries about the deeds or actions that you committed as evidence against you. Since you are holding yourself to a higher standard, you will need to be very tough.

Take a look at the evidence and examine it closely then become the toughest prosecutor against yourself. You will have to be the prosecutor and the judge, then eventually plead for leniency and seek mitigation. It is advisable to be strict and harsh sometimes should the need arise.

As the experts say, changing bad habits can be pretty difficult because most people are unaware of the bad habits in the first place. Let's say you skip work and choose to stay at home and watch TV instead. This is pretty bad behavior that should be nipped in the bud as soon as possible. As a person seeking to better yourself and bring out the best in yourself, you need to be conscious of your actions and the impact these habits or actions have on others. If there is a bad habit, then investigate it. Try to be strict and find out exactly what is causing the bad behavior. If there is a root cause, then this should be addressed. This is all about training your mind so that you think in the right way.

Chapter 5: Master the Art of Tranquility with Stoic Techniques

Peace of mind is another extremely popular tenet that the stoics spoke of in great depth. People are always seeking peace and tranquility. Peace of mind is considered the great thing, and it is according to the words that Seneca said to his friend Serenus.

Peace of mind is also known as tranquility. There are plenty of people around the world who may be successful in numerous ways but do not have peace of mind. This tends to happen for various reasons. There are those who are challenged by their goals because they are inconsistent in their goals. They keep changing their minds then regretting it almost immediately.

Some people may seem fickle but rather suffer due to their dullness. They tend to live their lives based on inertia—in the very same way they started out—instead of living the way they please. Many other people think that traveling far and wide provides the solution to ensure a life devoid of boredom and dullness. However, even when they travel, they get to carry their problems with them. As such, travel does not bring peace and tranquility.

As the stoics say, all individuals try to flee from themselves. However, as they discovered, our problems are not domiciled where we dwell but within ourselves. This, therefore, means that we cannot run away from ourselves but should deal with our issues in order to lead a peaceful and tranquil life. As such, we need to pause and examine our lives, then find a solution to why we are not at peace.

One of the best ways of attaining peace of mind is to focus on your actions by executing the duties of a citizen and participating in the management of the affairs of a nation. According to Seneca, being of service to others and the nation not only keeps you occupied but also ensures that you become a useful member of society.

It also pays to do good to society and still focus on reading and understanding philosophy. This is because it is what Seneca and other stoics did most of the time. They took care of their personal and business matters, participated in the affairs of the nation, and also studied philosophy. Philosophy is not simply a narrow field of study; it opens up the mind and leads a person to a much freer, open, and tranquil life. People leading such lifestyles enjoy much satisfaction and hence the peace of mind and tranquility that they enjoy.

There are others who do not enjoy life but live to a ripe old age. Such old people may not have much to show for their lives but will only be old without being able to prove the quality life that they lived. Retirement in life is necessary but should be done at a slow pace so that people may also be able to continue being of use to society by providing essential services. Also, people need to keep practicing virtue no matter what because virtue is a prerequisite for tranquility. Even in an oppressive regime, it is possible for a person to lead a decent and noble life doing good to others, participating in affairs of the state, and being a decent member of society. This shows that tranquility is possible regardless of the times that one lives in.

Sometimes people think they can provide more than they can or achieve more than they can. However, wisdom dictates that we all have limitations and that some of the things that we pursue are simply not worth the effort. Life is short and our time on this earth is limited, so it is advisable to only focus on matters that are important to us and crucial to our wellbeing. We need to apply ourselves to matters and issues that we can complete within a reasonable time and at a reasonable pace.

As a person, you need to be careful about the people that you associate with. This means interacting with people who add value to your life and not those who take away things from you. Also, we need to ensure that we devote our time and effort to those worthy of our time and energy. We need to engage in pursuits that bring us joy and satisfaction as much as possible. Working on things or projects that you do not enjoy adds little value and is viewed as a struggle against nature.

Property and possessions sometimes turn out to be the things that cause us the most pain. As it is, both the rich and poor handle these matters in the same way. All suffer the same way. Even men with hair and those without are suffering because of wealth and possessions. An opinion, however, is that it is okay to be wealthy and own property, but we should not get attached to our property. Some stoics, such as Diogenes, owned no property just to avoid the conflict that comes with it. Others, like Seneca, were wealthy and owned property.

In the latter part of his life, Seneca advised us to get rid of most properties that we own so we do not get too attached to them. Fundamentally, people who keep only minimal property will be happier, especially if they do not get too attached to their possessions.

We also need to be able to adjust appropriately to new situations. In life, our situations change sometimes. For instance, we may lose all that we have, and we may lose a friend or loved one and so on. This happens all the time; however, we should teach ourselves or learn how to move one from such happenings in order to maintain a good quality life.

Stoicism and Tranquility

According to stoics, we are all mortal beings, and one day we will all transition to the next life. Also, life is never easy, and we all experience different challenges. It may sound sad, but all the people that you know will one day pass away. These are the facts of life. The important aspect is determining how you will spend your time and how you will live your life. We also go through some painful experiences and life is full of hardships. Some people are likely to go through painful periods in their lives including prolonged difficulty and extreme pain.

The reality is that we could lose our loved ones or our lives at any time. Accidents happen, and incidents occur. These could change our lives drastically. Also, we could spend time, effort, and years of hard work building something only to have it taken away or broken down. However, to lead peaceful and tranquil lives, we should not hope that these things do not happen. Instead, we should focus on living a good quality of life in a world where death and hardships are a reality.

People often wonder whether it is possible to lead a happy and tranquil life. You will see many people simply put down their heads and cope. They bear the hardships and just accept whatever comes their way. We tend to live like death and hardships do not exist because we like to ignore them. This is not the best way to live, though, as we are then forced to face hardships and life's challenges unprepared. A different approach is necessary.

The practice of ancient stoicism can help us to lead a happy and tranquil life. It is not a good idea to live life as if hardships, challenges, and death do not happen. Stoicism provides the lessons and tools necessary for a peaceful life even in a world full of death and hardships.

Lessons from stoicism

There are crucial lessons that we can all learn from the early stoics. These lessons are important in helping us live peaceful, fulfilling and tranquil lives. Stoicism offers a way for us to have a clear perspective on life. This perspective is conducive with happiness and inner peace.

Stoic philosophy focuses on numerous aspects of life. One of these is a principle that enables us to have an understanding of control. Stoicism also focuses on enabling us to have a different and suitable perspective on our lives. Stoicism also teaches us about the tools we need to use to handle sadness and suffering should life deal us a tough blow.

Stoics' notion of control

In life, there are things which we can control and those that we cannot. We all know of numerous things in our lives that we have no control over. For instance, you park your car, then leave only to find someone hit it and caused damage. Or perhaps you are a victim of an unexpected illness that devastates you. These events do happen in life and are often out of our control.

According to stoics, most of the things that happen in your life are generally outside of your control. This means you do not have control over most of the things that happen to you. However, there are instances where you do have control over your life. For instance, you do have control over your body and the kind of food that you eat. Eating healthy and taking care of your body will ensure that you live a healthy life that is largely disease-free and thus you will live for many years.

Eating healthy regularly, working out, and going to sleep early are some of the things that we have control over and which can improve the quality of our lives. Fate does determine some things though, such as who our parents are, our genders, countries where we are born, and so on.

According to Epictetus, some of us will be born with amazing talent while others will be born with disabilities and will achieve almost nothing in life. The rest of us will lead average and mundane lives with little or no achievement to show for it. This is generally what occurs everywhere around the world and is a fact that should be acceptable.

Fate also causes some of us to be born into wealthy and successful families while others are born with great genetics, talents, and so on. But according to stoics, there are certain things that we can control, and if we do a good job, we will emerge victorious and successful in life.

There are events in life that we can control. For instance, we can attend interviews and work hard to succeed, and we can also eat well and exercise daily to avoid illnesses. This means that in order to have peace of mind, we must give our best in everything that we do or say. It is like students sitting an exam. Such students should not worry or fret about the outcome of the exam. All that they need to do is ensure that they work hard and perform to the best of their ability. This way, they will not have to worry even if they do not pass the exam.

Tranquility lies in the fact that a person has done his or her best in everything. When you put in the time, effort, and resources, that is all that is required of you. The rest of it is beyond you. Stressing over things that are beyond your control is not advisable and will not help you. Instead, take heart knowing that you did all that you could do and the rest is beyond your control.

Take the example of the sun shining up in the sky. You would never worry that it will not rise. In fact, stressing over such things only stresses you out. Therefore, learn to do your very best and work hard, then the rest of it will most likely fall in place. And even if it does not, you will still have done your best and that is the most important thing.

Chapter 6: Stoic Principles to Smash Creative Blocks

What does the term creativity mean? We know that it is among the most fundamental of all our human characteristics. Others are our social instincts and reasoning capacity. Creativity can be defined as the process of bringing into a life a concept, idea, image or anything else that was not previously in existence. This is a human activity that can be employed at any time. It could be as simple as sending an email, preparing a meal, writing a song or even making amends.

Stoicism and creativity

Stoicism has a lot to do with creativity. When you put the two together, you combine the creative process with the appropriate way of living. The principles of stoicism lead us to have much more purpose in everything that we do and apply ourselves to the best of our abilities. If you follow these principles, then you will become an accomplished creator with a greater purpose. You will also approach life with a lot more meaning, purpose, and appreciation.

Marcus Aurelius is one of the leading stoics who introduced most of the stoic principles and stoicism philosophy. In one of his teachings, he teaches us to give ourselves wholeheartedly to the arts and crafts that we have learned and not to be a tyrant or slave in order to be happy. As human beings and creatives, we have to provide service to our fellow human beings, especially in the roles that we play in this world. If you are creative, then you should engage yourself the best you can in order to give and produce your very best.

As individuals, we can uphold and cultivate a life that generally flows smoothly. When it comes down to it, a stoic is simply any person who transforms mistakes into initiation, fear and pain into reason, and personal ambition into action. A stoic therefore is any person who wants the upside of life without the downside.

Creative works

There are all forms and sorts of creative work. They could be in the form of business, paintings, books, and so much more. There is something that all these have in common too—success for any creative work boils done to saying something, finding a suitable way to say it, and a receptive audience. Creativity is all about creating a new thing in the hope that others will like it so that you may keep at it. Being creative can be an intimidating and lonely affair that is full of self-doubt and fear. Stoicism can help creatives to overcome these challenges.

- Spend your time with the right kind of people

We become the average of the five people that we spend the most time with. As such, it is important for writers, singers, actors, and other creatives to spend more time hanging around people that inspire and educate them. If you hang around people that push you to become better, then you are definitely going to become a better person and a more accomplished artist.

There are plenty of examples of how this theory works. Take Johann Wolfgang van Goethe for instance. His maxim states that he can tell whom you are based on the people that you hang around the most. Also, a man named Austin Kleon, who was an artist and poet, said that most of the people in history that we view as geniuses were actually part of a larger group of individuals who supported, inspired, and encouraged each other. In short, a genius is not necessarily an individual but an ecosystem.

Therefore, be very careful about the kind of people that you let into your life. This is because these individuals will have a huge impact on it and your productivity. Make sure that the people who come into your life will push you forward, encourage you, motivate you, and occasionally hold you accountable.

- *Always be early to rise*

There are probably numerous times when you struggle to wake up in the morning. Sometimes you do not feel like waking up on time and spend a couple of minutes, or even hours, snoozing. However, you are creative, and your work influences many people. You need to keep in mind the fact that you wake up early in the morning to produce useful content that the world desperately needs. Remember that you are in this world to serve a purpose and accomplish your mission. Snoozing or sleeping in can be extremely enjoyable. We derive pleasure when we extend our sleeping times by a couple of minutes. However, we were not created for pleasure but to serve humanity and accomplish a purpose.

Think about Mondays and how people hate them. We find it hard to wake up early Monday morning to go to work or to fulfill other responsibilities that we have. However, this is not really strange because over 2,000 years ago the emperor of Rome was struggling with the same problem. The challenge of waking up early begins when we first attend school at an early age. This continues into adulthood until retirement.

It always feels nice to steal a couple more minutes and snooze. However, as a creative, you should avoid this as much as possible. You have a crucial task to undertake—to come up with works of art that the rest of the world will appreciate. To really be creative and successful, you need to be up early and engage your creative mind. Therefore, as soon as it is time to wake up, make sure that you get up, get out of bed, hit the shower, and have your cup of morning coffee.

- *Your intentions should always be clear*

As a creative, do not be ambiguous. All your efforts and hard work need to be aimed at accomplishing a definite goal. Having a goal does not necessarily mean that you will achieve it. However, when you have no goal in sight, then you will definitely not achieve it.

Stoics advise us never to have false or unattainable conceptions. These are usually the main cause of depression, worry, and stress. They are also responsible for dysfunctional and chaotic lives. Your efforts have to be directed towards a definitive purpose and cause; otherwise, you will simply be operating day in and day out without any direction. It will not be possible to have a purpose, know when to stop, and so on.

The lesson here is that you have to define exactly what your purpose is and what you are all about. Let your intentions stand out and be clear to all.

- Always assess yourself accurately

According to Seneca, we all need to periodically assess ourselves and come up with a true, accurate, and reasonable estimate of ourselves. This is because we often tend to assume that we can do much more than we really can.

Plenty of people reject the idea of self-assessment because it will most likely reveal their true worth, which is something they are not prepared to accept. However, even though we may not be willing to receive news about our less than impressive assessment, it is crucial that the assessment is done. You should not be scared of the self-assessment simply because you may not like the outcome. It is much more damaging to you when you fail to assess yourself and overvalue your capabilities. A lot of the time people underestimate their capabilities but on few occasions overestimate that of others.

As a creative, you need to develop the culture of self-assessment and do so accurately yet honestly. Examine yourself, understand your capacity and capabilities, and also discern what you are capable of achieving and what you cannot.

- Encourage and maintain your good habits

Epictetus once said that all habits and capabilities grow based on a corresponding action. For instance, you can be a better runner if you practice running and make it a habit. Similarly, you will nurture a good trait by making it a habit.

The mind operates in the same manner. According to Aristotle, we become what we repeatedly do. For us to excel, therefore, we simply need to nurture a habit. Marcus Aurelius added to this by saying our character of mind is the result of our habitual thoughts.

What you first need to do is examine your activities for the past week, the past couple of days, and the present day. Also, examine the activities you have planned for the next week. Think about the person that you are or aspire to be. Are your planned activities in support of this person that you are or desire to be? What kind of person are you turning out to be?

- *Stoics and creatives are a work in progress*

According to the stoics, philosophy is never an end on its own. We all aspire to be better, to improve ourselves, and lead better, more successful, and more peaceful lives. No single individual in the world is sick, exiled, dying, or in danger and totally happy. This means that learning the principles of stoicism will not instantly transform your life. Instead, we need to transform our lives by getting better each day.

All the things that we learn through philosophy and principles of stoicism should be applied to our lives. These are things that we need to continue doing not for a while but a lifetime. When we keep applying the important tenets, then we keep improving. Simply put: we do not cease being stoics but continue getting better each day.

Chapter 7: Differentiate Things We Can and Can't Control

Epictetus is among the first and most popular of the early stoics. His teachings and wise words form the cornerstone of stoicism principles. Epictetus teaches us that the most fundamental task in life is to note the things that are external and beyond our control and those which we actually have control over. As such, it becomes easy to search for good and evil as these are within our control and the choices that we make.

The most crucial principle of the stoic philosophy is learning how to tell the difference between things within our control and those we cannot control. There are things that we have influence over, and then there are those beyond our influence. For instance, if you are flying to a different city, then you have control about getting yourself to the airport on time. However, things such as turbulence in the air, departure, and arrival times are all beyond your control. Therefore, you should focus on doing the things that are within your control.

Serenity

There is a special prayer known as the Serenity Prayer. This is a prayer that beseeches the Almighty to help handle the things within our control and accept the things beyond our control. This prayer will help you as you aim to lead a life that is devoid of unnecessary worry but allows you peace of mind:

"Lord, grant me the courage to change the things that I can change, the serenity to accept the things that I cannot change, and the wisdom to understand the difference."

This Serenity Prayer was originally authored by a US-based Christian teacher Reinhold Niebuhr in 1934. This prayer was consequently adopted by groups such as Alcoholics Anonymous and similar ones. This prayer helps different people accept the things they cannot change but then gives them the courage to do the things that they can in order to change the future.

Most people who face hardships as kids or other challenges in the past cannot do anything about this past. However, they can take action now and change the future to ensure that it is a bright one. This is done and accomplished through the power of the present moment. According to Epictetus, they have the power and ability to make changes in their lives right now.

This principle applies in many other situations. What we need to do is focus on articulating the sections of our days within our control and those that are not. We will enjoy happiness and peace of mind if we focus only on the things within our control and ignore the rest. If we can do this properly, then we will be better off compared to individuals who keep fighting battles that they cannot win or challenges they cannot overcome.

Fear is generally an emotion that can hold you back. However, if you realize that it is only an emotion just like any other, then you will be willing to take on more risks and consider all the financial, personal and professional risks available to you.

Focus

Always try and ensure that your goals are internal. If you are hoping for a promotion at work and you have to submit an application, then the best course of action is to update your resume and include all the relevant information. Include the experiences and skills gathered and any strengths you believe will support your application.

As a stoic student, once you submit your application believing you have done your level best, then there will be no need to worry. All that can be expected of you is to do your very best and then hope for a positive outcome. There is no need to worry unnecessarily. Also, there is no room for passive acceptance of things that occur to you. All that you need to do is completely accept the things that you cannot change and have no power over. Then focus and do your best where you have the power and influence to make a change.

Stoicism is not just limited to minor inconveniences in life. Some people have gone through traumatizing and life-altering experiences but have survived and emerged victorious by applying the stoic principles. It is similar to playing a game of tennis. When you play tennis, you want to win. The person who will win the match is not known and is beyond your control. However, there are some factors that you can control, such as how you play. You can only commit to playing the best tennis possible. That is within you, and the rest is beyond you.

Other factors that are beyond you include the person you want to love you, the weather, and so on. In fact, according to the stoics, there is very little that is within our control, and so if we can discern this, we will be happier and at peace. If you are active politically, you cannot necessarily determine which party will win elections. However, you can get active and become a political activist. This way you will possibly influence policy and perhaps even persuade others to vote for your party and your preferred candidates. In essence, you need to do what is within your control to the best of your ability. The rest you leave to fate or God.

Chapter 8: Control Emotions and Minimize Worry with Stoicism

A stoic is walking and comes across a bunch of kids. The kids stare at him, insult him, call him all sorts of names, then laugh at him. The stoic wishes them a nice day and walks away. This brief anecdote pretty much sums up what stoicism is all about.

Life is not easy, and the early stoics knew this for a fact. Many bad things happen, and they tend to affect a lot of people negatively. However, stoics taught people to be happy and cheerful, especially if the unhappiness was as a result of things beyond your control.

However, stoics also advised us to understand our capabilities and possibilities and not to overestimate our worth. If we get the true value of ourselves, then we will not overestimate our worth, and this will help us make the right decisions in life. You will be disappointed with life and not attain peace of mind or happiness if you overestimate your worth because life will most likely disappoint you.

Since bad things are likely to happen in this life, you should learn to accept them. This way, you will not be too disappointed when they occur as they are often beyond your control. Instead, learn to focus on things that you can control. There are a few things that are within your control so your focus should be on these. If you can handle the things within your reach and do the best that you can, then that is all that the universe will ever require of you.

Impossible expectations

Stoics declared that our emotions, especially negative emotions, are as a result of our overly-high expectations about life. People often expect a lot out of life. They think that life is supposed to be great, and successful, and full of nice people and nice things. Often, life is pretty difficult and challenging. People experience many troubles and hardships that their expectations end in disappointments.

The stoics stated that the best state of mind is where we instill virtue and also use our minds to reason and apply the reasoning in our lives in the best way possible. Basically, we should not let our emotions guide us, but we should always be rational in our thinking.

Let emotions take the back seat

It is not wrong to let our emotions get the better of us. Sometimes we let emotions take the driver's seat so that they guide our actions and reasoning. For instance, we need to get greed out of our lives and eat food more for nourishment and less of it for other reasons, such as health. We should not eat to fill an emptiness or void caused by our emotions. Also, it is not advisable to own too much property and other worldly possessions. These end up occupying your mind, and you begin worshipping them and losing focus. Owning things also leads to worry and this worry will distract you from more important things. According to the early stoics, there is no material possession necessary for a happy and successful life.

Stoics had certain tools necessary to live a happy life. One of these is negative visualization. According to their philosophy, this is a great approach if you want to get rid of emotions that cause you to worry and fret. Therefore, we should not focus on material possessions, and we should not worry about things beyond our control. Also, according to stoics, we should imagine or visualize the disaster should our possessions get lost. This is because we can expect to lose things dear to us sooner or later. By visualizing these things, then we can expect not to feel too bad when they eventually happen.

How to minimize worry and control your emotions

So how do you minimize worry and control your emotions? As discussed in the Introduction, there are certain practices and procedures. The most prominent of these are certain spiritual exercises that are greatly inspired by ancient writings. Different people approach stoicism differently, but the basic principles are the same across the board. Here are some common stoic practices.

The first activity of the day should be meditation. You should find a nice and quiet place where you can spend some moments meditating. The spot you choose should not be too brightly lit. It does not have to be outdoors but a spot even in your home that is comfortable and quiet.

As you meditate, take time to focus on your day ahead and think about the virtues and doctrines of stoicism. Sometimes stoics also focus on certain sayings from the ancient philosophers like Socrates. Read one or two and think about it then try and live according to the saying.

You first think about yourself and then extend the thoughts to your family, friends, and close circle. You also think about the residents of your city, your neighbors, and people where you work and live. You finally extend this circle and think about the people of this world, nature, and eventually the entire universe.

Also, take a view of yourself like before but this time from an aerial view. Expand this circle and also think about your country, the sky, clusters of galaxies, and the entire universe.

Anger and emotions

We have all experienced anger and emotions at some point in our lives. It is now evident to us that when we are angry, anxious, sad, or emotional, we never make any smart decisions or wise choices. Even when we are in love or mourning we basically unproductive without doing any useful work. In order to be calm, we require emotional stability.

Your thoughts often emanate from you. As such, you are a product of your thoughts. According to the stoics of the ancient, we are all products of our reasoned decisions. This is because our thoughts are the only thing that we totally and fully control. As such, we may not be our thoughts, but the outcome of these thoughts or the product is definitely us.

The same case applies to the brain. We are not actually our brains, but we are the master or CEO of the brain. This is because we do not necessarily control all that goes on there, but we can determine which activities we are going to focus our energies on. Therefore, if something is worrying or bothering your mind, simply ask yourself if these thoughts are worth your time or energy.

If you have reason to be concerned based on the nagging thought, then, by all means, do something about it. However, if everything appears to be great and the thought does not warrant your time and energy, then discard the thoughts without spending any precious time or effort.

Anger emanates from the feeling of entitlement

When we get angry, it is often because we feel that we are entitled to something. Often reality fails to conform to our wishes or desires and this sets us off. There are plenty of things that tick us off. It could be traffic, a careless motorist, delayed payments, and so on. Always ask yourself if the world owes you anything.

Take the instance of a huge traffic jam, and you urgently need to get somewhere. Unfortunately, traffic does not allow you to move, so you get angry. However, according to stoics, traffic should never be a source of anger or other emotions. At least that is what this world owes you. In the same manner, imagine a situation where someone does not keep your promise but fails you instead. You may feel that you have a right to get angry and that people should keep their promises.

However, someone failing to keep their promise should not cause you to be angry. This is because we know that human beings are weak and often fail to keep their promises. As such, we need not have high expectations even when they make promises. Therefore, do not get angry because someone did not keep their promise. You may hold them to account and call them out but never fall into the anger trap.

You do not need certain possessions to be happy

Often, people believe that they need certain possessions to be happy. Scores of people around the world have a lot less than what you have. Many of these people lead happy lives, and they are content with what they have. If everything were all about money, then countless people around the world who have almost none would be extremely sad and dejected, which is not the case.

Also, there are lots of people who have one form of disability or another. Others have lost loved ones or suffered from other tragedies, yet plenty of them are rather happy and content with life. If such people can be happy with very little possessions and some serious handicaps, then it means you can live with whatever you do not have. The more things you need to be happy, the more miserable your life will be.

Therefore, the next time you want something but do not get it, you should ask the question "Is this thing necessary?" or "Do I really need it" or "Can I do without it?" Let's say you have a career in law, banking or accounting. You hope for a promotion at work in the shortest time possible. However, you should ask yourself whether a promotion right now will make you happy. In most cases, you will find that you can lead a pretty happy life without a promotion. As such, it is not a necessary ingredient for your happiness. With this outlook, you should be able to avoid feeling sad, angry, dejected, and worried. All that you need to be happy is within you. All the rest are not necessary, and you can do well without them.

Chapter 9: Stoicism and Cognitive Behavioral Therapy

Some unfortunate people suffer from anxiety and panic attacks. Most victims of this condition often seek treatment and therapy from mental health experts. Many of these patients claim that they will never forget the first panic attack. The heart pounds really fast while the face turns white. Adrenaline courses throughout the body.

Philosophy and cognitive behavioral therapy

According to Socrates, philosophy also happens to be a kind of talking therapy. Stoicism philosophy does constitute a form of therapy and a kind of medicine for our minds. As such, philosophy, and especially stoicism, is viewed as a form of psychotherapy.

Stoicism emphasizes the use of philosophy as a form of mental therapy. In fact, according to Epictetus, it is better that the soul receives therapy rather than the body. This is because it is preferable to die rather than live a low-quality life. It is, therefore, amazing to listen to witnesses who have used stoicism philosophy as a form of therapy to cure their anxiety and panic attacks.

This is what happened to the author Jules Evans. He used to suffer serious bouts of anxiety and panic attacks for many years. Then one day he came across stoicism philosophy and what it says about inner peace, happiness, and all its other principles. He got his health, peace of mind, and normal life back after applying the principles of stoicism.

Return to health and happiness

While many therapists make use of medication and other forms of treatment, it is only after some patients made use of stoicism philosophy that they got completely healed. Stoicism actually forms the basis of modern cognitive behavioral therapy.

The CBT theory made its first appearance in the city of Athens in 350 BC. Back then, stoics used to teach their followers at the marketplaces. Their teachings were philosophical but very practical as well. Stoicism teaches us how to control and understand our emotions. We do not need to stifle our feelings but should instead learn how to be in control again. If we are in control of our emotions, then we will be able to handle negative emotions and overcome their effects on us.

Negative emotions happen, and they tend to make us feel helpless. They result in conditions like anxiety, depression, and panic attacks. Fortunately, stoics are very aware of these emotions. They are basically not a result of external stimuli but our thought process. For instance, we get anxiety and panic attacks not because of all the people in the room staring at us but because of the thoughts in our minds. Mental challenges like these are usually as a result of our numerous thoughts. It is our beliefs that give us our mental problems. Moreover, it is crucial that we understand the source of the worry, stress, anxiety, and panic attacks are from within and not without. Sometimes we think it is other people's thoughts of us or their opinions that cause us the mental issues, but this is not the case.

According to stoics, negative emotions in us are usually the result of some external thing that we are constantly or regularly attached to. For instance, we are so concerned about the opinion of other people about us. This is crucial, and it is important to keep this in mind. When we focus our attention and base our happiness on external things, then we will never be content, happy or secure.

The best approach, according to the stoics, is to focus on what is within our control. And what we have control over are our thoughts and the thought process. As an individual, when you follow the teachings of the stoics, you will eventually learn to become your own master and become the master of things that you can control. This will save you from the problem and stress of being a slave to what other people think about you.

Chapter 10: Inspiring Stories from Popular Stoic Followers

Stoics measure success using various parameters. These include virtue, peace of mind, learning and applying lessons learned, and so on. They have also learned to make the right decisions that are in tandem with nature and never against it. As long as this is the case, then stoics are not really bothered by the outcomes. If they end up as a disabled person, then they are happy—it is the same case if they turn out to be extremely wealthy and successful. Their happiness is not based on possessions but more on being at peace and accepting things that they cannot change.

Stoicism provides a solution for living an excellent life regardless of a given situation or even stage in life that one is at. People are made to think and consider what things are honorable, decent, and truly important so they can apply what is decent and honorable.

Stoicism is designed deliberately to add value to life, to be actionable, and to make sense. In fact, no one needs to learn any new meditation techniques or philosophical theories. Stoicism simply offers practical, beneficial, and instant ways of improving a person's character and finding peace and tranquility in simple yet practical ways.

Here are some brief but inspiring stories about successful individuals who learned the stoic philosophy for peace of mind and happiness. They applied the relevant principles in their lives and enjoyed immense success based on a stoic lifestyle:

1. Ryan Holiday

Ryan Holiday is a US-based entrepreneur, marketer, and popular author. He is also a staunch stoicism follower and has written widely about his stoic experience. His latest book is titled, *The Obstacle Is the Way*. This book talks about many things but also speaks about his stoic experience and how stoic principles have led him to become the successful writer and marketer that he is today.

Ryan dropped out of college at nineteen and went into business. He had been a student at the University of California where he studied both creative writing and political science. He learned and studied writing under the famous author Robert Greene. Greene wrote the book, *The 48 Laws Of Power*, which is an all-time best seller.

Ryan has authored numerous books, many of which have also become best sellers. He has written for well-known and renowned newspapers and magazines including *The Guardian, Forbes, The New York Observer, The Huffington Post,* and *Fast Company.*

Apart from authoring books and writing for renowned publications, Ryan has spoken, written, and given lectures about stoicism. Many people appreciate his views on stoicism and have come to accept the stoicism philosophy as part of their lives. His works have been noted specifically by *The New York Times* as having significantly popularized stoicism.

2. Timothy Ferris

Tim Ferris is an American author who studies stoicism. He is also a best-selling author and has twelve books published, all of which have won acclaim. His book *Coming of Age in the Milky Way* was nominated for three Pulitzer Prizes and won a prize at the American Institute of Physics.

Many years after completing his studies in Miami, Ferris became a writer and wrote for many renowned organizations. He was at one time an editor at *Rolling Stone*. He later worked as a consultant for NASA and provided advice and guidance to the organization on matters relating to space exploration policy.

Ferris is a successful man now in retirement. His success was largely brought on by his adherence to stoic principles. He is a well-known stoic follower and believer. He has gone on to earn numerous honors in his life including Fellow of the American Association for the Advancement of Science. He is also a Guggenheim Fellow.

His other accomplishments include being a university professor and lecturer. He has taught philosophy at university and other subjects including history, English Literature, and journalism.

3. Rear Admiral James Stockdale

James Stockdale was a member of the US Military and an admiral in the US Navy. Stockdale was an outstanding serviceman who fought in Vietnam, held there as a war prisoner for seven years, and awarded the Medal of Honor which is considered a significant achievement for services rendered to the nation.

While serving in the military, Stockdale won numerous other awards including two Bronze Star medals, the Distinguished Flying Cross, the Silver Star, and the Navy Distinguished Service Medal. He undertook his military studies at the Naval Academy before he was dispatched to the Vietnam War. He retired from the military in 1979 and began his writing career. In the same year, he became the president of the Naval War College.

He went on to become a successful businessman and candidate for the vice presidency of the United States. His stoic beliefs and principles saw him become a successful military leader, businessman, accomplished soldier, and so much more. Stockdale says that stoicism helped him survive as a prisoner of war.

4. Pete Carroll

Pete Carroll is an American football coach who headed the Seattle Seahawks in the National Football League (NFL). He has coached other teams in the same league including the New England Patriots and the New York Jets. He is among very few elite coaches of the NFL who have won both college football national championships as well as the Super Bowl.

Carroll started his coaching career in 1973 when he was in his early twenties. He started out as a graduate assistant at Pacific under Chester Caddas. In 1984, he became the coach of the Buffalo Bills and focused on the defensive backs. He soon rose to become a full-time coach. His success as a coach came through his stoicism beliefs. He instilled the same in his players who also became quite successful.

5. President Theodore Roosevelt

Finally, we can take a look at the life of President Theodore Roosevelt. He was also many other things, including a conservationist, a sportsman, a statesman, and a writer. Roosevelt was the US president who served between 1901 and 1909. Prior to that, he served as vice president of the USA from March to September 1901.

He was an avid adventurer, a writer, and student of stoicism. He explored sections of the Amazon River in South America that many had never explored. He also went on numerous excursions to Africa on Safari. He spent many hours reading about the stoics. And like all other followers, he applied what he learned as a stoic to his life.

Chapter 11: Complete Stoic Guide for Perfect Health

The Ancient Greek stoic philosophers have taught us much about living a stress-free life with peace of mind. Their teachings also provide us with numerous lessons regarding life, our emotions, and thoughts. Some may wonder if philosophers can teach us about good health and what to eat. However, just looking at the American diet, it is possible to see the biggest influencers in the past half a century or more.

Stoicism provides lots of lessons on indifference to death, strong emotions, self-sufficiency, and taciturnity. When it comes to disease and illnesses, some of their principles are at the forefront. Here is a look at stoicism and health.

Stoicism and health

In the first century AD, there lived a man named Musonius Rufus. Rufus was a stoic philosopher who lived during the reign of Emperor Nero. However, the emperor exiled him like he did numerous other philosophers. While he is not as well-known as others, Rufus is among the early stoic philosophers. He is best known for advancing the teachings of Epictetus.

According to Rufus, living a virtuous life almost equates to living a healthy life. He believed the two went hand in hand in as much the same way as we respect others and ourselves. His works got so popular that several other stoics started paying attention to his teachings—the philosophy of eating begun gaining traction and has been popular ever since.

According to Rufus, health and strength are better than physical pleasure which makes us slaves of the stomach and weak. One of their strong points was to insist on fasting occasionally. Fasting helps to boost our self-control especially when it comes to matters of the stomach. Rufus taught his students that when you have self-control in drinking and eating, then you will have laid the foundation of temperance. He also emphasized on the need to be the master when it comes to matters of food and appetite in order to overcome greed and master self-control.

Basically, according to the stoics, there is definitely nothing wrong with eating nutritious foods. In fact, nutrition is crucial for a healthy body and normal functioning of the body. Stoics were miles ahead when it came to food and nutrition.

Anyone who views food as a source of pleasure and enjoyment is probably unaware of the challenges this poses to them. Without self-control, we turn to addictive foods, including sweets, fatty foods, and all manner of unhealthy foods. These foods tend to be addictive like that of illicit drugs. Sweet and sugary foods often affect the pleasurable and addictive sections of the brain. These are the same sections of the brain affected by addictive drugs like cocaine and marijuana.

Basically, when we consume large amounts of unhealthy foods, we are setting ourselves up for addiction and other challenges. These foods are dangerous and should at best be avoided. Stoics were very aware of this even as early as two thousand years ago.

Eat nourishing foods

As stoic followers, there are certain things that we can learn from this. We need only to consume healthy and nourishing foods. We also should avoid unhealthy foods eaten for pleasure only. When we fast and avoid addictive foods, we basically eat more for nourishment than pleasure. This way, we learn to develop self-control and conquer greed. We become responsible for our bodies and take charge of our health.

It is advisable to follow the eating patterns and habits of the stoics rather than politicians and others. Remember that stoics were all about detachment from status and wealth. They appreciate the simple pleasures of life and resist anything that suggests comfort while accepting some basic circumstances. For purposes of peace of mind and a good life, it is advisable to seek peace, genuine fulfillment, and gratification.

State your life's purpose and repeat it often

The stoics believe in living a life full of purpose. This is a life built around serving others, being humble, accepting life and what it has to offer, doing our best where we have control and living a simple life.

Basically, where we invest most of our moments is where we invest our lives. Ensure that you align yourself to your purpose in life each day. Do not put that off on the guise of addressing other pressing needs. If you do not watch out, these other pressing needs will become your life. You can be happy and content with what you have if you follow stoic principles. Some people are content with what they are, and others are happy with what they have.

It is crucial that we focus on health every day. We can only live a purposeful life if we are healthy. We also need to be virtuous individuals and people of integrity. Integrity requires us to be real in what we do and what our choices are. Our choices should align with our purposes and integrity should be at the core. We need to ask of ourselves each day the kind of people we aspire to become.

Always be grateful

It is important to learn to be a person of gratitude. Being a grateful person in all ways is crucial and will make you a better person. Always remember that life is essentially a careful balance of negative events and positive situations. According to the stoics, we should align ourselves to neither in order to have serenity or peace of mind.

Some people complain every day, arguing that everything is wrong and nothing is working out. They never view the positive aspect of things and also struggle with things that are beyond their control. We learn that numerous things in life are beyond our control. Accepting these things rather than getting mad and upset gives us peace of mind. Getting mad and complaining robs us our peace of mind and tranquility.

As it is, we all have something to be grateful for each day. This is because if we look closely, we note that every person receives something every day. We receive good things which we should be happy about. Having a job, a good boss, some food to eat, a loving family, and a warm home to go to are things to be grateful about.

Live within set boundaries

When we talk of boundaries, we don't mean actual walls but to set certain limitations. We operate as human beings within certain limitations and limited resources. Also, our time and energy are very limited. If we do not acknowledge this, then we will not be successful.

Think about your investments, friends, and even relationships. Think about which ones are important to you and serve a useful purpose—these are the ones that you should focus your energies and resources on. We cannot afford to be friends with everyone and foster numerous relations, some of which may be unhealthy for us. Instead, we should focus on important relationships that add value to our lives. We can then let the rest go. Setting such limitations will lead you to have a more meaningful life.

Learn to detach from certain issues and let go

There are times when we want something, but we do not get it. We end up losing out. There are many things that we desire in life. Sometimes we acquire what we want, and sometimes we do not. If we get too attached to these things, then we lose out because we become angry, dejected, stressed out, and sad. However, we can learn to detach ourselves from all these things, especially life's pleasures and material possessions.

Become a disciplined person

Most people today are pretty soft. Life provides us with many comforts such as air conditioning, tap water, grocery stores, digital devices, and so much more. We really do not have to sweat a lot about things such as walking and transporting goods, fetching groceries, and so on. As such, our bodies have grown "soft" and we are not in touch with a tough, physical body.

We should learn to get out of our comfort zones and engage in activities that expose us to much of what goes on around the world. We should learn to interact with others, including less fortunate members of society. This kind of exposure will help us appreciate what we have and help us to get in touch with reality.

Have a grip on what you can control

The stoics taught us how to live a life of acceptance. We should accept the things that happen to us that are beyond our control. There are plenty of things we have control over but only very few that are beyond us. As such, we need to focus on the things we can control and then ensure that we do our best in relation to these things.

Most of the time people get mad and furious at things beyond their control. They get angry when they do not get something that they really wanted. Yet this is not the best approach. Practice accepting things that are beyond your control no matter how much you wanted them. This way, you will always have peace of mind.

Also, learn to accept that your life is like a loan. In life, we do not have indefinite time. We cannot afford to lead our lives any way we like. We should understand our lives have a time limit and we should focus on living our best lives possible. Avoid procrastination, eat healthily, lead a virtuous life, do your best with the things you have control over, and accept things you have no control over. If you do this, then you will live a happy life with contentment and peace of mind.

Conclusion

Thank you for making it through to the end of this book. It should have been informative and provided you with all of the tools you need to achieve your goals, whatever they may be.

This book also should have opened your eyes to stoicism and its amazing principles. Many people in America, Europe, and around the world are adopting the stoics' way of living and applying its teachings. You too can apply the stoic philosophy to your life if you wish to find more happiness, peace of mind, and tranquility.

Stoicism has been around for years, and the principles put forth have been confirmed to be true, accurate, and valid to this day. For instance, we can be happy if we learn to detach ourselves from earthly possessions and pleasures. We can also attain peace of mind by accepting things beyond our control and doing our very best on the little that we have control over.

Plenty of successful individuals around the world have had success in their careers while following stoic principles. They include successful writers, authors, football coaches, scientists, and even presidents. Many of them have written about their experiences and how stoicism has helped them attain the success that they enjoy.

Finally, if you found this book useful in any way, a review on Amazon is always appreciated!

Made in the USA
Coppell, TX
22 August 2021